Connections

Level 5

Authors

Rosalind Ragans, Ph.D., Senior Author

Willis "Bing" Davis   Jane Rhoades Hudak, Ph.D.   Bunyan Morris
Tina Farrell   Gloria McCoy   Nan Yoshida

Contributing Author

Jackie Ellett

ART
SOURCE
RCE
ARTSOURCE

Education Division
The Music Center of Los Angeles County

Columbus, OH

The **McGraw·Hill** Companies

Authors

Senior Author
Dr. Rosalind Ragans, Ph.D.
Associate Professor Emerita
Georgia Southern University

Willis "Bing" Davis
Associate Professor Emeritus
Central State University - Ohio
President & Founder of
SHANGO: The Center for the
Study of African American
Art & Culture

Tina Farrell
Assistant Superintendent
Curriculum and Instruction
Clear Creek Independent
School District,
League City, Texas

Jane Rhoades Hudak, Ph.D.
Professor of Art
Georgia Southern University

Gloria McCoy
Former President
Texas Art Education Association
Spring Branch Independent
School District, Texas

Bunyan Morris
Art Teacher
Effingham County School
System, Springfield, Georgia

Nan Yoshida
Art Education Consultant
Retired Art Supervisor
Los Angeles Unified School
District
Los Angeles, California

SRAonline.com

Send all inquiries to:
SRA/McGraw-Hill
8787 Orion Place
Columbus, OH 43240-4027

Printed in the United States of America.

ISBN 0-07-601824-5

1 2 3 4 5 6 7 8 9 RRW 10 09 08 07 06 05 04

Contributors

Contributing Author
Jackie Ellett
Elementary Art Teacher
Duncan Creek Elementary School
Hoschton, Georgia

Artsource® Music, Dance, Theatre Lessons
Mark Slavkin, Vice President
for Education, The Music Center of
Los Angeles County
Michael Solomon, Managing Director
Music Center Education Division
Melinda Williams, Concept Originator and
Project Director
Susan Cambigue-Tracey, Project Coordinator
and Writer
Madeleine Dahm, Movement and Dance
Connection Writer
Keith Wyffels, Staff Assistance
Maureen Erbe, Logo Design

More about Aesthetics
Richard W. Burrows
Executive Director, Institute for Arts
Education
San Diego, California

Safe Use of Art Materials
Mary Ann Boykin
Director, The Art School for Children and
Young Adults
University of Houston—Clear Lake
Houston, Texas

Museum Education
Marilyn J. S. Goodman
Director of Education
Solomon R. Guggenheim Museum
New York, New York

Resources for Students with Disabilities
Mandy Yeager
Ph.D. Candidate
The University of North Texas
Denton, Texas

Music Connections
Kathy Mitchell
Music Teacher
Eagan, Minnesota

Student Activities

Cassie Appleby
Glen Oaks Elementary School
McKinney, Texas

Maureen Banks
Kester Magnet School
Van Nuys, California

Christina Barnes
Webb Bridge Middle School
Alpharetta, Georgia

Beth Benning
Willis Jepson Middle School
Vacaville, California

Chad Buice
Craig Elementary School
Snellville, Georgia

Beverly Broughton
Gwinn Oaks Elementary School
Snellville, Georgia

Missy Burgess
Jefferson Elementary School
Jefferson, Georgia

Marcy Cincotta-Smith
Benefield Elementary School
Lawrenceville, Georgia

Joanne Cox
Kittredge Magnet School
Atlanta, Georgia

Carolyn Y. Craine
McCracken County Schools
Mayfield, Kentucky

Jackie Ellett
Duncan Creek Elementary School
Hoschton, Georgia

Tracie Flynn
Home School
Rushville, Indiana

Phyllis Glenn
Malcom Bridge Elementary
Bogart, Georgia

Dallas Gillespie
Dacula Middle School
Dacula, Georgia

Dr. Donald Gruber
Clinton Junior High School
Clinton, Illinois

Karen Heid
Rock Springs Elementary School
Lawrenceville, Georgia

Alisa Hyde
Southwest Elementary
Savannah, Georgia

Kie Johnson
Oconee Primary School
Watkinsville, Georgia

Sallie Keith, NBCT
West Side Magnet School
LaGrange, Georgia

Letha Kelly
Grayson Elementary School
Grayson, Georgia

Diane Kimiera
Amestoy Elementary School
Gardena, California

Desiree LaOrange
Barkley Elementary School
Fort Campbell, Kentucky

Deborah Lackey-Wilson
Roswell North Elementary
Roswell, Georgia

Dawn Laird
Goforth Elementary School
Clear Creek, Texas

Mary Lazzari
Timothy Road Elementary School
Athens, Georgia

Michelle Leonard
Webb Bridge Middle School
Alpharetta, Georgia

Lynn Ludlam
Spring Branch ISD
Houston, Texas

Mark Mitchell
Fort Daniel Elementary School
Dacula, Georgia

Martha Moore
Freeman's Mill Elementary School
Dacula, Georgia

Connie Niedenthal
Rushville Elementary
Rushville, Indiana

Barbara Patisaul
Oconee County Elementary
School
Watkinsville, Georgia

Elizabeth Paulos-Krasle
Social Circle Elementary
Social Circle, Georgia

Jane Pinneau
Rocky Branch Elementary School
Watkinsville, Georgia

Marilyn Polin
Cutler Ridge Middle School
Miami, Florida

Michael Ramsey
Graves County Schools
Paducah, Kentucky

Rosemarie Sells
Social Circle Elementary
Social Circle, Georgia

Jean Neelen Siegel
Baldwin School
California

Debra Smith
McIntosh County School System
Darien, Georgia

Patricia Spencer
Harmony Elementary School
Buford, Georgia

Melanie Stokes
Smiley Elementary School
Ludowici, Georgia

Rosanne Stutts
Davidson Fine Arts School
Augusta, Georgia

Fran Sullivan
South Jackson Elementary School
Athens, Georgia

Kathy Valentine
Home School
Burkburnett, Texas

Debi West
Rock Springs Elementary School
Lawrenceville, Georgia

Sherry White
Bauerschlog Elementary School
League City, Texas

Patricia Wiesen
Cutler Ridge Middle School
Miami, Florida

Deayna Woodruff
Loveland Middle School
Loveland, Ohio

Gil Young
Beverly Hills Middle School
Beverly Hills, California

Larry A. Young
Dacula Elementary School
Dacula, Georgia

Table of Contents

▲ **Jaune Quick-to-See Smith.**
Spam.

Unit 1 Line, Shape, and Value

◀ **Jan Vermeer.**
The Concert.

Unit 2 Space, Shape, and Form

◀ **Lavina Fontana.**
Portrait of a Noblewoman.

Unit 3 Color and Pattern

◀ **Viola Frey.**
Grandmother Series:
July Cone Hat.

Unit 4 Proportion and Distortion

◄ **Vincent van Gogh.**
House at Auvers.

Unit 5 Texture, Rhythm, Movement, and Balance

▲ **Berthe Morisot.**
The Sisters.

Unit 6 Harmony, Variety, Emphasis, and Unity

Technique Tips

Activity Tips

Visual Index

What Is Art?

Art is . . .

Painting is color applied to a flat surface.

▲ **Vincent Van Gogh.** (French). *Houses at Auvers.* 1890.

Oil on canvas. $29\frac{3}{4} \times 24\frac{3}{8}$ inches (75.56 × 61.93 cm.). Museum of Fine Arts, Boston, Massachusetts.

Drawing is the process of making art with lines.

▲ **Pablo Picasso.** (Spanish). *Portrait of Dora Maar.* 1938.

Pencil on paper mounted on fiberboard. $30\frac{9}{16} \times 22\frac{7}{16}$ inches (77.62 × 57 cm.). Hirshhorn Museum and Sculpture Garden, Smithsonian Institution, Washington, D.C.

Sculpture is art that fills up space.

▲ **David Bates.** (American). *Seated Man #4.* 1995.

Painted wood. $88 \times 37\frac{1}{2} \times 45\frac{1}{2}$ inches (223.52 × 95.25 × 115.57 cm.). Dallas Museum of Art, Dallas, Texas.

Architecture is the art of designing and constructing buildings.

▲ **Jørn Oberg Utzon.** (Danish). *Opera House.* 1957–1973.

Sydney, Australia.

Printmaking is the process of transferring an original image from one prepared surface to another.

▲ **Katsushika Hokusai.** (Japanese.) *Winter Loneliness,* from *One Hundred Poems Explained by the Nurse.* 1839.

Woodcut. $10\frac{1}{16} \times 14\frac{1}{2}$ inches (25.5 × 36.8 cm.). Honolulu Academy of Art, Honolulu, Hawaii

Photography is the act of capturing an image on film.

◀ **Eliot Elisofon.** (American). *Asante Paramount Chief Nana Akyanfuo Akowuah Dateh II, Akwamuhene of Kumase.* 1970.

Photograph. National Museum of African Art, Smithsonian Institution, Washington, D.C.

Ceramics is the art of making objects with clay.

▲ **Artist Unknown.** (Kongo peoples, Congo and Democratic Republic of Congo.) **Bowl.** Late-nineteenth to early-twentieth century.

Ceramic and resin. $5\frac{7}{8} \times 4\frac{1}{8} \times 5\frac{7}{8}$ inches (14.9 × 10.49 × 14.94 cm.). National Museum of African Art, Smithsonian Institution, Washington, D.C.

A mask is a covering for the face to be used in ceremonies and other events.

▲ **Charlie James.** (Southern Kwakiutl.) *Sun Tranformation Mask.* Early nineteenth century.

Royal British Columbia Museum, British Columbia, Canada.

Art is created by people

▶ to communicate ideas.

▶ to express feelings.

▶ to give us well-designed objects.

What Is Art?

Every work of art has three parts.

Subject

The objects you can recognize are the subject matter of a work of art. When a work has no recognizable objects, the elements of art such as lines, shapes, colors, and so on become the subject of the work.

Composition

The composition of the work is the way the artist has used the principles to organize the elements of art.

Content

The content is the message the artwork communicates. Content is the meaning of the work. If the work is functional, such as a chair or clothing, then the content is the function of the object.

▶ In which work of art do you think the subject matter is very important?

▶ In which artwork do you think composition is most important?

▶ Which work seems to have the strongest message? Explain.

▶ Which artwork's meaning relates to its function?

▲ **Benny Andrews.** (American). *Grandmother's Dinner.* 1992.

Oil on canvas. 72 × 52 inches (182.88 × 132.08 cm.). Ogden Museum of Southern Art, New Orleans, Louisiana.

▲ **William Sharp.** (English/American). *Great Water Lily of America.* 1854.

Chromolithograph on woven white paper. $21\frac{1}{4}$ × 27 inches (53.98 × 68.58 cm.). Amon Carter Museum, Fort Worth, Texas.

▲ **Artist Unknown.** (Maya/Huipil). *Huipil Weaving.* c. 1950.

Backstrap woven plain weave with supplementary-weft pattern, silk on cotton. 50 × $14\frac{1}{2}$ inches (127 × 36.83 cm.). Museum of International Folk Art, Santa Fe, New Mexico.

▲ **Mosche Safdie.** (Israeli). *Habitat.* 1967.

Concrete. Montreal, Canada.

Subject Matter

Artists make art about many subjects. *Subject matter* is the content of an artist's work. For example, the subject of a painting can be a vase of flowers or a self-portrait. This subject matter is easy to see. The subject matter is harder to understand when the artwork stands for something beyond itself. Look at the artwork on these pages. Notice the different kinds of subject matter.

Still Life

▲ **Paul Cézanne.** (French). *Still Life with Basket of Apples.* 1895.
Oil on canvas. $23\frac{3}{5} \times 31\frac{1}{2}$ inches (60 × 80 cm.). The Art Institute of Chicago, Chicago, Illinois.

Landscape

▲ **Z. Vanessa Helder.** (American). *Rocks and Concrete.* c. 1940.

Watercolor on paper. 19 × 15$\frac{7}{8}$ inches (48.26 × 40.34 cm.). Cheney Cowles Museum, Spokane, Washington.

What Is Art?

Genre

▲ **Winslow Homer.** (American.) *Nooning.* c. 1872.

Oil on canvas. $13\frac{5}{16} \times 19\frac{5}{8}$ inches (33.02 $\times$ 48.26 cm.). Wadsworth Atheneum, Hartford, Connecticut.

Nonobjective

◀ **Natalya Goncharova.** (Russian). *Maquillage.* 1913.
Gouache on paper. $4\frac{3}{8} \times 6\frac{3}{8}$ inches (11.13 × 16.21 cm.). Dallas Museum of Art, Dallas, Texas.

Portrait

◀ **Elizabeth Catlett.** (American). *Sharecropper.* 1970.
Color linocut. 26 × 22 inches (66.04 × 55.88 cm.). Smithsonian American Art Museum, Washington, D.C.

What Is Art?

Allegory

▲ **Jan van Eyck.** (Flemish.) *Portrait of Giovanni Arnolfini and His wife Giovanna Cenami.* 1434.
Oil on wood panel. 32 x 23 inches. The National Gallery, London, England.

Symbolism

▲ **Artist Unknown.** (Huichol People/Mexico). *Mother of the Eagles.* 1991.
Braided yarn embedded in vegetable wax on wood. $15\frac{3}{4} \times 19\frac{1}{2}$ inches (40 × 49.53 cm.). Private collection.

Elements of Art

Art is a language. The words of the language are the elements of art.

Line

Shape

Form

Space

Color

Value

Texture

Principles of Art

Artists organize their artwork using the principles of art.

Pattern

Rhythm

Balance

Emphasis

Harmony

Variety

Unity

About Art

▲ **Frida Kahlo.** (Mexican). *Frida y Diego Rivera.* 1931.
Oil on canvas. $39\frac{3}{8} \times 31$ inches (100.01 $\times$ 78.74 cm.). San Francisco Museum of Modern Art, San Francisco, California.

Look at the artwork.

▶ What people or objects do you see?

▶ Do they look like people and objects you see around you today? Explain.

Look at the caption.

▶ When was the artwork created?

▶ What can you learn about the artist?

Learn more.

▶ Do some research to find out more about the artist, the artwork, and the time period.

About Art

▲ **Frida Kahlo.** (Mexican). *Frida y Diego Rivera.* 1931.
....
Oil on canvas. 39⅜ × 31 inches (100.01 × 78.74 cm.). San Francisco Museum of Modern Art, San Francisco, California.

Look

▶ Look at the work of art. What sounds, smells, or feelings are in this work of art?

▶ What happened just before and just after in this work of art?

▶ What kind of music would be playing in this work of art?

Look Inside

▶ Imagine you are one of these people. Who are you? What are you thinking? How do you feel?

▶ If you could add yourself to the painting, what would you look like? What would you be doing?

▶ Act out or tell the story in this work of art with a beginning, a middle, and an end.

▶ Draw what you can't see in this work of art. Are there hidden images that should be revealed?

Look Outside

▶ How is this like or different from your own world?

▶ What does the artist want you to know or think about in this work of art?

▶ Describe your journey in viewing this work of art. Include your thoughts, ideas, and changes in thinking.

▶ What will you remember about this work?

About Art

▲ **Frida Kahlo.** (Mexican). *Frida y Diego Rivera.* 1931.
••
Oil on canvas. 39⅜ × 31 inches (100.01 × 78.74 cm.). San Francisco Museum of Modern Art, San Francisco, California.

Art Criticism

Describe

▶ List everything you see in this painting. Be sure to describe the people and their clothing.

Analyze

▶ How has the artist used line, shape, color, value, space, and texture?

▶ What kind of balance has the artist used?

▶ Has the artist used emphasis to make us notice one thing more than others?

Interpret

▶ What is happening?

▶ What is the artist telling us about these two people?

Decide

▶ Have you ever seen another artwork like this?

▶ Is it successful because it is realistic?

▶ Is it successful because it is well-organized?

▶ Is it successful because you have strong feelings when you study it?

About Art

▲ **Frida Kahlo.** (Mexican). *Frida y Diego Rivera.* 1931.
. . . .
Oil on canvas. $39\frac{3}{8} \times 31$ inches (100.01 $\times$ 78.74 cm.). San Francisco Museum of Modern Art, San Francisco, California.

How does an artist create a work of art?

Art is a process. You can follow the same steps to create your own work of art.

1. Get an idea.

▶ Artists get inspiration from many places. Look around you. People, objects, and scenes may provide inspiration for a work of art.

2. Plan your work.

▶ Do you want your artwork to be two-dimensional or three-dimensional?

▶ Decide what media you want to use.

▶ What materials will you need?

3. Make a sketch.

▶ Think about how you want your artwork to look. Sketch several ideas.

▶ If your artwork will be three-dimensional, sketch it from different points of view.

▶ Then choose the best idea.

4. Use the media.

▶ Make an artwork based on your best idea. You may want to practice using the materials first.

▶ When making your composition, remember the elements and principles of art. How can you use them to make your artwork say what you want it to say?

5. Share your final work.

▶ Evaluate your work using the four steps of art criticism. What do you like best about your work? What would you do differently next time?

Safety

► Use art materials only on your artwork.

► Keep art materials out of your mouth, eyes and ears.

► Use scissors and other sharp tools carefully. Keep your fingers away from the cutting blades.

► Wash your hands after using the art materials.

► Wear an art shirt or smock to protect your clothes.

► Use only art materials with a "nontoxic" label.

- ▶ Return art materials to their proper storage place.
- ▶ Be careful not to breathe chalk or clay dust.
- ▶ Use only new and clean foam trays.
- ▶ Do not walk around the room with sharp tools in your hand.
- ▶ Be aware others in your work space.
- ▶ Always follow your teacher's directions when using the art materials.

Line, Shape, and Value

▲ **Jaune Quick-to-See Smith.**
(American). *Spam.* 1995.

Acrylic and mixed-media on canvas.
60 × 100 inches (152.4 × 254 cm.).
Private collection.

Line, shape, and value are used by artists to create many types of art.

Jaune Quick-to-See Smith used many kinds of lines, a variation of dark to light color, and both geometric and natural shapes to direct the viewer's eyes across *Spam.* She used contour drawing to emphasize the shape of the buffalo. This piece communicates our responsibility to our environment.

Artists use the element of **line** in works of art to create movement and shapes.

▶ What area of the picture do your eyes see first? What do you see last?

▶ What types of lines do you see? Do you see any of these lines more than once?

The element of **shape** is used by artists to create objects and people.

▶ What shapes do you see in this painting?

In This Unit you will learn about and practice how artists use line, shape, and value to create art. Here are the concepts you will study:
▶ Types of lines
▶ Shape
▶ Value

Jaune Quick-to-See Smith

(1940–)

Jaune Quick-to-See Smith grew up on a Montana reservation. Her Shoshone grandmother gave her the name "Quick-to-See" because she was quick to understand things. As a child, she often went on long trips with her father, who was a horse trainer and trader. She saw the rugged beauty of the Northwest's landscape and was inspired to draw. Smith's paintings reflect her concern for preventing the destruction of the environment and for the preservation of Native American cultures.

Lesson 1

Expression with Lines

Look at the artwork on these pages. The *Huipil Weaving* is part of a garment made and worn by the Cakchiquel Maya of Guatemala. In *Convergence,* Jackson Pollock created overlapping lines by dripping and sometimes splattering paint while moving in a dancelike motion around the canvas on the floor. Lines are used in both pieces of art to create mood and movement.

◀ **Artist Unknown.** (Maya/Huipil). *Huipil Weaving.* c. 1950.

Backstrap woven plain weave with supplementary-weft pattern, silk on cotton. 50 × 14½ inches (127 × 36.83 cm.). Museum of International Folk Art, Santa Fe, New Mexico.

 ## Art History and Culture

How have these artists expressed their culture through these works of art?

▲ **Jackson Pollock.** (American). *Convergence.* 1952.

Oil and enamel on canvas. $93\frac{1}{2} \times 155$ inches (237.49 × 393.7 cm.). Albright-Knox Art Gallery, Buffalo, New York.

Study both works of art to find a variety of lines.

▶ Do you see a line that zigzags?

▶ Which lines are curved?

▶ How do the lines help to create a mood?

▶ Compare the two works of art. Do you see lines that are similar?

🔍 **Aesthetic Perception**

Design Awareness Look around the classroom for various types of lines. What kinds of lines do you see in the furniture?

Using Lines

A **line** is a mark drawn with a tool such as a pencil, pen, or paintbrush as it moves across a surface. Lines have different lengths, widths, and textures. Some curve and move in different directions.

 Vertical lines move up and down, creating a feeling of strength and stability.

 Horizontal lines move from side to side, creating a calm feeling.

 Diagonal lines move at a slant and express movement.

 Zigzag lines are made by joining diagonal lines.

 Curved lines bend and change gradually or turn inward to form spirals.

Lines can be long or short, thick or thin, and rough or smooth.

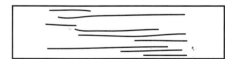  

Practice

Use lines to create a pose.

1. Choose a line type from above.

2. Draw an example of this line type on one side of a note card, and write what type of line it is on the other side.

3. Together with your assigned group, create a pose that displays the lines each of you has drawn on your note cards.

4. Pose in front of the class while the other students try to identify the lines your group has used.

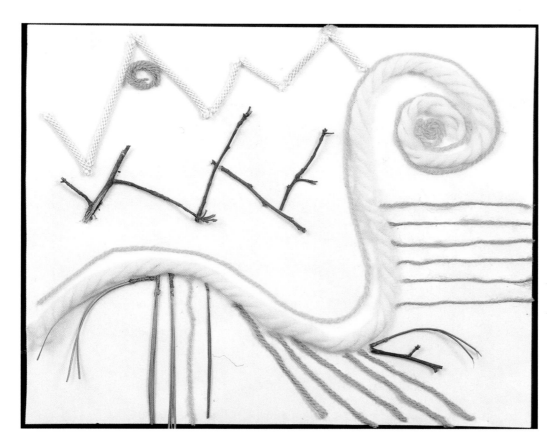

Think about the types of lines the student artist used in this mixed-media collage.

Creative Expression

In what ways can you make lines besides drawing them? Create a mixed-media collage using lines.

1. Think about the five different types of lines. Collect linear mixed-media materials such as yarn, string, and grass.

2. Use different materials to create lines and line variations. Keep in mind the mood that certain lines suggest.

3. Arrange and glue the collage materials onto a piece of cardboard.

Art Criticism

Describe What materials did you use in your collage?

Analyze How did you use lines to express a mood in your collage?

Interpret What title would you give the collage?

Decide Were you successful in communicating the feelings that you wanted to express? If you could do this collage over again, how would you change it?

Perception Drawing

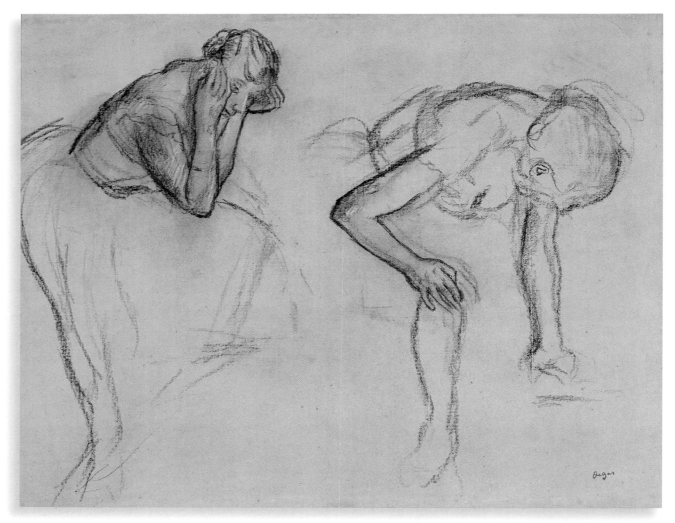

▲ **Edgar Degas.** (French).
Ballerinas. 1885.

Charcoal and chalk on paper.
18 × 23½ inches (45.72 × 59.69 cm.).
High Museum of Art, Atlanta, Georgia.

Look at the artwork on these pages. Notice how both artists used lines to show how the people in the artwork are moving. Notice that Degas did not erase the extra lines on the ballerina's arm. Toulouse-Lautrec finished the woman's head but left the rest of her body sketched.

 Art History and Culture

How did these European artists express their French culture through these works of art?

▲ **Henri de Toulouse-Lautrec.**
(French). *Madame Thadée
Natanson at the Theater.* 1895.
. . . .
Gouache on cardboard. 24½ × 29½ inches
(62.23 × 74.93 cm.). The Metropolitan
Museum of Art, New York, New York.

Study both works of art to find examples of
gesture and contour drawing.

▶ Where do you see gesture drawing in these works
of art?

▶ Where do you see contour drawing in these works
of art?

▶ Find a repeated gesture line that represents
movement.

▶ Can you see a beginning or an end to the
contour lines?

Aesthetic Perception

Design Awareness How would you use contour lines to draw a
classroom object? How would it appear in a gesture drawing?
Which drawing seems more fitting for representing this object?

Using Perception in Drawing

Perception drawing is looking at something carefully and thinking deeply about what you see as you draw.

The **contour** of an object or figure is its edges and surface ridges. Artists often make contour drawings of objects and use them as studies before making a painting or drawing.

Contour lines are continuous, unbroken lines that show the edges and surface ridges of an object.

Gesture lines are drawn quickly to capture the movement of a person, animal, or object in a painting or drawing.

A **gesture sketch** is a drawing that tries to capture the gesture or movement of an object as quickly as possible. Unlike a contour drawing, a gesture sketch will show what the artist sees inside the object's outline.

Practice

Use a gesture sketch to capture movement.

1. Look at the subjects who are posing. Notice the lines and shapes.
2. Quickly sketch what you see. Try to capture the feeling of movement by using repeated lines.
3. Do not spend time drawing a lot of detail.
4. Share your gesture sketch with the class.
5. Identify the use of lines that show movement in the sketches.

Think about how the student artist used one continuous line to draw the subject posing.

🎨 Creative Expression

How can you improve your perception, or the way you look or think about what you see? Create a contour drawing of subjects.

1. Look carefully at the posed subjects.

2. Move your pen slowly on your paper while your eyes move around the edges or contours of the subjects.

3. Look at the subjects while you draw, and only glance occasionally at your paper.

4. Do not pick up your pen. Draw in one continuous, unbroken line.

❗? Art Criticism

Describe Did you draw your lines using the proper procedure?

Analyze Did you use one continuous, unbroken contour line?

Interpret What mood do the lines in your drawing create?

Decide Were you successful in concentrating on the edges and surface ridges of what you saw and re-creating that on paper?

Lesson 3

Geometric and Free-Form Shapes

▲ **Georges Braque.**
(French). *Still Life on Red Tablecloth.* 1936.

. . . .

Oil on canvas. $38\frac{1}{4} \times 51$ inches
(96.52 × 129.54 cm.). The Norton
Museum of Art, West Palm Beach,
Florida.

Look at the artwork on these pages. In Paul Cézanne's *Still Life with Basket of Apples,* the viewer sees the table arrangement from one point of view. Georges Braque's *Still Life on Red Tablecloth* gives the viewer a chance to see the scene from many points of view. Both works of art have **geometric shapes** and **free-form shapes.**

 Art History and Culture

Which of these still-life works of art is abstract?

44 Unit 1 • Lesson 3

▲ **Paul Cézanne.** (French).
Still Life with Basket of Apples. 1895.

Oil on canvas. $23\frac{3}{5} \times 31\frac{1}{2}$ inches (60 $\times$ 80 cm.).
The Art Institute of Chicago, Chicago, Illinois.

Study both works of art to find a variety of shapes.

▶ Where do you see geometric shapes in these works of art? Describe them.

▶ Which objects have free-form shapes?

▶ Point to the solid shapes made with color and those created with outlines.

Aesthetic Perception

Seeing Like an Artist Turn a book in your hands. How many shapes can you see as you look at it from different angles?

Using Geometric and Free-Form Shapes

Shapes are two dimensional and can be measured by height and width. A shape can have an outline or boundary around it, or it can be solid like a shadow. Geometric and free-form are two kinds of shapes.

Geometric shapes are shapes that can be described in mathematical formulas, and they have names. The three basic geometric shapes are the square, the circle, and the triangle. When you combine these shapes you create **complex geometric shapes** such as those below.

Parallelogram

Trapezoid

Pentagon

Hexagon

Octagon

Free-form shapes are uneven and irregular. They can be made with curved lines, straight lines, or a combination of the two. They are found most often in nature.

Practice

Create complex geometric shapes. Use paper cutouts.

1. Cut out basic shapes such as circles, squares, and triangles from paper.

2. Experiment with the cutout shapes to create complex geometric shapes.

Think about how the student artist created mood with shapes.

Creative Expression

How can you create a still life by using the computer as a drawing tool?

1. Think about objects you might enjoy drawing. Select five or more different sizes and shapes.

2. Arrange the still life. Look for shape, color, and lines.

3. Using a computer, open the paint program and practice using the tools that you will use to draw your still life.

4. Using the paint program, draw the still life. Save and print your finished product.

Art Criticism

Describe What objects did you draw?

Analyze How did you use lines and color to create shapes?

Interpret Is your work calm or exciting?

Decide Were you able to use a variety of shapes in the still life that you arranged?

Value with Hatching

▲ **Elizabeth Catlett.** (American).
Sharecropper. 1970.

. . . .

Color linocut. 26 × 22 inches
(66.04 × 55.88 cm.). Smithsonian American
Art Museum, Washington, D.C.

Look at the artwork on these pages. Both Catlett's *Sharecropper* and Whistler's *Weary* are portraits. Catlett created *Sharecropper* by cutting hatching lines into linoleum. These lines appear to be white on the printed page. Whistler scratched lines into a metal plate to create value changes. Hatching was used to show changing value in both pieces.

 Art History and Culture

Look at the women in these works of art. Use context clues such as their clothing and the title of the artwork to decide what they are looking at.

Study both works of art to find a variety of lines.

▶ What types of lines do you see?

▶ Where are lines close together or far apart?

▶ Which areas have dark values and which have light values?

▶ What feelings does each work express?

◀ **James McNeill Whistler.**
(American). *Weary.* 1863.
· ·
Drypoint. $41\frac{1}{5} \times 27\frac{1}{8}$ inches (105.4 × 69 cm.).
National Gallery of Art, Washington, D.C.

Aesthetic Perception

Design Awareness Look at comic strips in the newspaper for examples of hatching used to show value.

Using Hatching to Create Value

The darkness or lightness of an object refers to its **value.** Line patterns create different values. When lines are placed side by side, or parallel, value is created. The closer together parallel lines are, the darker the value. The farther apart the lines are placed, the lighter the value.

Hatching creates shading values by using a series of fine parallel lines.

Cross-hatching creates shading values by using two or more intersecting sets of parallel lines.

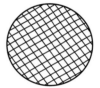

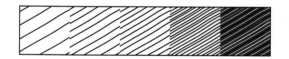

Practice

Using parallel lines, draw a value scale. Use a pencil.

1. Draw a rectangle and divide it into five sections.

2. Draw parallel lines far apart in the section to the left to show the lightest value. Gradually draw lines closer together until the far-right section, where the lines should be as close as you can get them without having them touch. In this way you will show the darkest value on the right side.

◀ **Lisa Kim.**
Age 10.

Think about how the student artist used hatching to show value.

Creative Expression

How can you use value to indicate form? Draw one or more models.

1. Sketch the models carefully.
2. Use hatching and cross-hatching to indicate value and form.

Art Criticism

Describe How many people did you draw?

Analyze How did you use hatching and cross-hatching to create value and form?

Interpret What mood does your work express?

Decide Does the use of hatching and cross-hatching make your sketch look more realistic?

Value with Blending

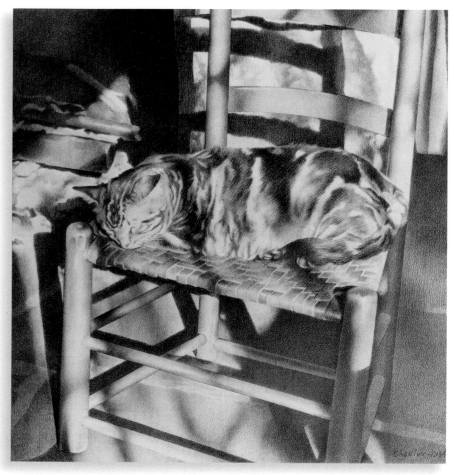

▲ **Charles Sheeler.** (American).
Feline Felicity. 1934.

Black crayon on paper. 22 × 18 inches (55.88
× 45.72 cm.). Harvard University Art Museums,
Cambridge, Massachusetts.

Look at the artwork on these pages. *Feline Felicity* is a portrait of a lounging cat in which Sheeler re-created the image by **blending** the light and dark values. This blending emphasizes the shadows and highlights cast by the sun. In *Study of a Sleeping Woman,* Rivera also used blending to help portray a realistic image of the woman.

 Art History and Culture

Both works of art were created during the same century. In which century were they created?

▲ **Diego Rivera.** (Mexican). *Study of a Sleeping Woman.* 1921.

Black crayon on off-white laid paper. $24\frac{1}{2} \times 18\frac{1}{2}$ inches (62.7 × 46.9 cm.). Harvard University Art Museums, Cambridge, Massachusetts.

Study both works of art to observe how values are created.

▶ Find the light and dark areas in both drawings.

▶ How have the artists used blending to create variations in value?

▶ Where did the artists use gradual blending?

▶ Where do you see a sudden contrast in value?

▶ What mood is suggested by the gradual blending of value in the artwork?

Aesthetic Perception

Seeing Like an Artist How would you draw a corner where the walls meet the ceiling? Would you blend the value gradually, or would the contrast between light and dark be drastic?

Using Blending for Value

Value describes the lightness or darkness of an object. Value depends on how much light a surface reflects.

Blending is the gradual change from one value to the next.

Practice

Experiment with value using colored liquid.

1. Dip the bottom of a coffee filter into a pan of colored water.
2. Allow enough time for the water to soak into the filter.
3. Notice where the value of the color is the darkest and how it gradually blends to a lighter color.

Think about how the student artist used blending to show realism.

 Creative Expression

How can you show realism with blended values? Use blended values to sketch an object.

1. Choose one or more common classroom objects.

2. Notice how much light the surface of these objects reflects. Look for shadows and variations of value.

3. Make line drawings of the objects.

4. Use blending to add form.

 **Art Criticism**

Describe Describe the object you included in your drawing.

Analyze In what areas have you blended the value?

Interpret How does blending affect the mood of the piece?

Decide Were you successful in creating blended values? What might you do to improve your drawing?

Value Contrast

▲ **Paul Strand.** (American).
From the Viaduct, 125th St.
1916.

Platinum print. 9$\frac{15}{16}$ × 13 inches
(25 × 33.02 cm.). Amon Carter Art
Museum, Fort Worth, Texas.

Look at the artwork on these pages. Both photographers used strong value contrast to tell a story about an American scene. In his cityscape *From the Viaduct, New York,* Paul Strand used natural light and shadows as well as the contrast of light- and dark-valued objects. Ansel Adams reprinted *Aspens, Northern New Mexico* in 1976 to strengthen the **value contrast.** He used a deep-yellow filter to create an effect that looks more like natural sunlight.

 Art History and Culture

How have these American artists expressed both similarities and differences within American settings?

▲ **Ansel Adams.** (American). *Aspens, Northern New Mexico.* 1958. Print 1976.

$17\frac{7}{8} \times 22\frac{5}{8}$ inches (43.18 × 55.88 cm.). Museum of Modern Art, New York, New York.

Study both works of art to see the values that were created.

▶ Where are the darkest and lightest values in each photograph?

▶ Do you see any areas where a bright light is next to a shadow?

▶ How did each artist use value to create a mood?

 Aesthetic Perception

Seeing Like an Artist Look around you. Are there areas of strong light next to dark, shadowed areas, like the ones in the photographs?

Using Value Contrast

The darkness or lightness of an object is its **value.** Value depends on how much light a surface reflects. Contrast is often created when working with values. **Contrast** is the degree of difference among color values, tones, shapes, and other elements in works of art. Using shading techniques such as stippling, cross-hatching, and hatching lines can help create value contrast in a drawing.

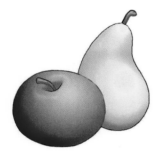 **Contrast** is the degree of difference among color values, tones, shapes, and other elements in works of art.

 **Cross-hatching** is when two or more sets of parallel lines cross each other to create value.

 **Hatching** is using a series of repeated parallel lines to create value.

 **Stippling** is shading with dots. The closer the dots are, the darker the area is.

Practice

Practice creating contrast in a drawing. Use a black marker.

1. Divide a sheet of paper into three sections. Label each section a shading technique: hatching, cross-hatching, and stippling.

2. Draw a different shape in each box and practice the different shading techniques.

◀ **Shavonta Johnson.**
Age 11.

Think about how the student artist has shown value contrast in the photograph.

Creative Expression

Where do you see value contrast in your environment? Take a photograph that has both bright highlights and dark shadows. Create a scene in such a way that it tells a story or expresses a mood.

1. Look around your indoor and outdoor environment. Find an interesting area, with objects or people, that tells a story or expresses a mood.

2. Use a camera. Look through the viewfinder to arrange your composition. Be sure that your photograph will have bright highlights and dark shadows. Take your photograph.

3. Have your photograph developed. Share it with the class.

Art Criticism

Describe Describe the objects and spaces you included in your photograph.

Analyze Does your photograph have highlights and shadows? Where are they? Do your values change gradually or quickly?

Interpret Give your photograph an expressive title.

Decide Were you successful in creating a photograph that has strong value contrast and also tells a story or expresses a mood?

Line, Shape, and Value

▲ **Raoul Dufy.** (French).
Open Window, Nice. 1928.
....
Oil on canvas. $25\frac{5}{8} \times 21\frac{1}{8}$ inches (65.1 × 53.7 cm.).
Art Institute of Chicago, Chicago, Illinois.

Art Criticism Critical Thinking

Describe What do you see?

During this step you will collect information about the subject of the work.

▶ What does the credit line tell you about the painting?

▶ What do you see in this painting?

▶ What is in the background?

Analyze How is this work organized?

Think about how the artist has used the elements and principles of art.

▶ Where do you see vertical, horizontal, diagonal, and curved lines?

▶ Where do you see geometric shapes and free-form shapes?

▶ Where are the darkest values and lightest values in the painting?

▶ Where do you see cross-hatching?

Interpret What is the artist trying to say?

Use the clues you discovered during your analysis to find the message the artist is trying to show.

▶ Who do you think lives in this room? Describe the person, saying as much as you can deduce from this room. What does he or she read? What music does he or she like?

▶ What do you think this room is used for?

Decide What do you think about the work?

Use all the information you have gathered to decide whether this is a successful work of art.

▶ Is this painting successful because it is realistic, because it is well-organized, or because it has a strong message? Explain.

Show What You Know

Answer these questions on a separate sheet of paper.

1 A _____ is a mark drawn by a tool as it moves across a surface.
A. dot
B. line
C. stippling

2 _____ are shapes that can be described by mathematical formulas.
A. Free-form shapes
B. Hatching
C. Geometric shapes

3 _____ refers to the lightness or darkness of an object.
A. Sketching
B. Curved
C. Value

4 _____ is the gradual change of one value to the next.
A. Blending
B. Zigzag
C. Value

5 _____ is the degree of difference among color values, tones, shapes, and other elements in works of art.
A. Stippling
B. Contrast
C. Cross-hatching

LET'S VISIT A MUSEUM
The Art Institute of Chicago

When it was originally established in 1879, The Art Institute of Chicago was called the Chicago Academy of Fine Arts. Today its membership reaches 150,000, the highest of any art museum in the country. Its collection has more than 225,000 works of art. There are ten different departments and galleries. The museum is known for its architectural displays and collection of French impressionist works. A large part of the museum is a school. People from all over the world attend classes in photography, painting, fashion design, and other visual arts.

▲ **The Art Institute of Chicago**

Line, Shape, and Value in Theater

Voice of the Wood is a play that has been adapted from a book. The story begins with a *luthier* (a maker of musical instruments) who crafts a cello from the wood of an ancient tree. The play tells the story of his quest to discover the touch that will unlock the "voice of the wood."

What to Do Write a story that could be turned into a play.

1. Write a short story that has a musical instrument as the main character. The instrument character can have human traits and emotions, or, instead, it can be a key element in the story plot.

2. Think about the materials used in making the instrument you chose. For example, your story could begin with a reed. A reed in a clarinet, when combined with wind, produces the sounds of the music the clarinet makes.

3. Think of the characters, the setting, the problem, and how it can be solved.

4. Once your story is written, divide it into three to five scenes that can be acted.

5. Share your story with a partner.

▲ Robert Faust and Eugene Friesen. "Voice of the Wood."

Describe Describe the lines and shape of the instrument you are featuring.

Analyze Explain how you created a story that features an instrument.

Interpret What emotions did you give to the instrument you chose?

Decide Do you think you succeeded in writing a story that can be turned into a play?

Space, Shape, and Form

◀ **Jan Vermeer** (Dutch).
The Concert. 1665–1667.
Oil on canvas. $28\frac{1}{2} \times 25\frac{1}{2}$ inches
(72.39 × 64.77 cm.).
Isabella Stewart Gardner Museum,
Boston, Massachusetts.

Many artists use space, shape, and form in two- and three-dimensional works of art.

Jan Vermeer relied on the use of space, shape, and form to help him create realistic paintings. He used perspective techniques in *The Concert* to create the look of depth on a flat surface. He also creates the illusion of form, using shading techniques. This makes the people and objects in *The Concert* look realistic.

Space is used by artists in paintings and drawings to give the illusion of depth on a flat surface.

▶ Notice how the tiles on the floor get smaller as they move into the painting.

Artists use several techniques to create the illusion of **form** on a two-dimensional, or flat, surface.

▶ What did Vermeer do to create form and to make the people and objects look realistic in this painting?

In This Unit you will learn about and practice techniques to create the appearance of space on a flat surface. You also will learn about three-dimensional forms. Here are the topics you will study:
▶ Space
▶ Form
▶ Perspective
▶ Shading
▶ Architectural form

Jan Vermeer.
Detail, At the Procuress'. 1656.

Jan Vermeer
(1632–1675)

Jan Vermeer was an artist who was almost unknown until about one hundred years ago. He painted fewer than forty works of art. Little was written about his life, but his paintings show that he was one of the world's greatest artists. Vermeer was interested in how scenes of everyday life might look to a person who is standing a short distance away. He used texture, value, and shape in a way that makes a scene appear to have natural light. Vermeer was only forty three years old when he died.

Positive and Negative Shapes and Space

Look at Jasper Johns's lithographs, titled *Cups 4 Picasso.* They are examples of optical illusions. He has intentionally organized shapes to create a visual puzzle to interest the viewer. Johns likes to change a recognizable object to attract more attention to it. Notice the way he changed the face of the Spanish artist Pablo Picasso. Jasper Johns arranges shapes and uses color to add interest to his artwork.

Jasper Johns. (American). ▶
Cups 4 Picasso. 1972.

Lithograph. $14\frac{1}{8} \times 32\frac{1}{4}$ inches (35.56 × 81.28 cm.). Museum of Modern Art, New York, New York.

 Art History and Culture

Jasper Johns is a pop artist. Pop artists use objects and ideas from their popular culture in their artwork. What objects and ideas might you see in today's pop art?

Study both works of art to find examples of positive and negative space.

► What shapes do you see in each of the images in this series?

► How many shapes are in each view?

► What technique did Johns use to show which shapes are most important?

► What changes occur from one image to the next?

◄ **Jasper Johns.** (American). *Cups 4 Picasso.* 1972.

Lithograph. $14\frac{1}{8} \times 32\frac{1}{4}$ inches (35.56 × 81.28 cm.). Museum of Modern Art, New York, New York.

 **Aesthetic Perception**

Design Awareness Look at street signs on your way home from school today. Notice how negative and positive spaces are used to create symbols to communicate messages.

Using Positive and Negative Shapes and Space

The element of art that refers to the area between, around, above, below, and within objects is **space.** Shapes and forms exist in space. It is the air around the object. There are two types of space: positive and negative.

Positive space is the objects, shapes, and forms in a work of art.

Negative space is the empty space that surrounds objects, shapes, and forms. When there is a large area of negative space in an artwork, loneliness or freedom might be expressed.

Shape reversal is when an object, shape, or form is positive space in one image and then in another image becomes negative space. Johns's lithographs show space reversal.

Practice

Practice drawing profiles. Use a pencil.

1. Draw a profile of a classmate's head.
2. Turn your paper upside down and copy the profile backward, just as Jasper Johns did.

◀ **Eric Flynn.**
Age 10.

Think about where you see the negative space in the picture.

 Creative Expression

How can you see the shapes of negative space? Draw the negative spaces in a still life.

1. Arrange objects in a still-life pose that have large, interesting negative spaces, such as chairs or desks.

2. Look closely at the still life and find an area of it that you like. Draw what you see. Concentrate on the negative spaces around the objects.

3. Using markers, fill only the negative spaces with color. Leave the positive spaces white.

 **Art Criticism**

Describe What objects did you draw?

Analyze What shapes did you create when you colored the negative space? How do the positive and negative shapes differ?

Interpret How did reversing the positive and negative spaces affect your drawing?

Decide Were you successful in defining the negative space around your objects?

Space in Two-Dimensional Art

▲ **Winslow Homer.** (American). *Nooning.*
c. 1872.

Oil on canvas. $13\frac{5}{16} \times 19\frac{5}{8}$ inches (33.02 × 48.26 cm.).
Wadsworth Atheneum, Hartford, Connecticut.

Look at the two realistic paintings on these pages. Even though both are two-dimensional works of art, the artists successfully used techniques to make some things look farther away than others.

 Art History and Culture

What can you tell about American and French culture in the late 1800s from looking at these realistic works of art? In addition to the visual clues, the titles offer clues as well.

▲ **William Adolphe Bouguereau.**
(French). *The Nut Gatherers.* 1882.

Oil on canvas. $34\frac{1}{2} \times 52\frac{3}{4}$ inches
(86.36 $\times$ 132.08 cm.). The Detroit
Institute of Arts, Detroit, Michigan.

Study both works of art to find how space is used.

▶ Find an object that overlaps and covers a part of another object, creating depth in each painting.

▶ Find an object that appears larger in one place and then appears smaller in another place.

▶ Where do you see strong colors? Where do the colors look weaker?

▶ Find an object near the bottom of one of the paintings and something near the top. Which of these objects seems closer to you?

Aesthetic Perception

Seeing Like an Artist When traveling home from school today, look at your surroundings. Compare the objects nearer to you to those farther away.

Space in Two-Dimensional Art

Perspective techniques are used to create the feeling of depth on a flat surface.

 Overlapping When one object covers part of a second object, the first seems to be closer to the viewer.

 **Size** Large objects seem to be closer to the viewer than the small objects. Size is often used together with placement to show depth.

 **Placement** Objects placed in or next to the foreground seem to be closer to the viewer than objects placed in or near the background. Placement is often used together with size to show depth.

 **Detail** Objects with clear, sharp edges and many details seem to be closer to the viewer. Objects that lack detail and have fuzzy outlines seem to be farther away.

 **Color** Brightly colored objects seem closer to the viewer. Objects with pale, dull colors appear farther away.

 **Converging Lines** Parallel lines seem to move toward the same point as they move farther away from the viewer.

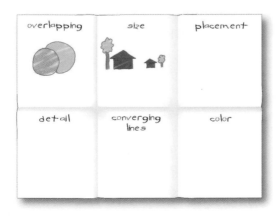

Practice

Illustrate each of the six perspective techniques. Use a pencil.

1. Fold your paper into six equal boxes. Print the name of a perspective technique in each of the boxes.

2. Draw an illustration for each technique.

◄ **Alison Thomas.**
Age 9.

Think about how the student artist used perspective techniques to paint an outdoor place.

Creative Expression

How can you use perspective techniques to create the illusion of depth? Paint a scene of a favorite outdoor place. Include depth.

1. Think of a place where you like to spend time outside.
2. Draw the scene with chalk, using at least three of the six perspective techniques.
3. Paint your scene.

Art Criticism

Describe Describe your outdoor scene.

Analyze What perspective techniques did you use to create depth in your two-dimensional painting?

Interpret Did you try to paint everything that you could remember in that outdoor area? If not, why did you choose to include some things but not others?

Decide Were you successful in creating the illusion of depth in your painting? Which perspective technique seems the most effective in creating depth?

Linear Perspective

Look at the artwork on these pages. Notice how the artists brought some objects in the paintings closer to the viewer and moved other objects farther away.

◄ **Childe Hassam.** (American). *Lower Manhattan (View Down Broad Street)*. 1907.
....
Oil on canvas. $30\frac{1}{4} \times 16$ inches (76.2 × 40.64 cm.). Herbert F. Johnson Museum of Art, Cornell University, Ithaca, New York.

 Art History and Culture

Which of these New York City scenes appears to be modern?

▲ **Frederick Brosen.** (American).
Watts Street. 1998.

Watercolor on paper. 30 × 47 inches
(76.2 × 119.38 cm.). Forum Gallery,
New York, New York.

Study both works of art to find perspective techniques.

▶ Follow the lines of the buildings and the streets that lead to the area that looks the farthest away.

▶ What types of shapes are repeated in each painting? How did the artist make some shapes appear farther away?

▶ Identify objects in the foreground, middle ground, and background in both paintings.

▶ Describe the use of detail in both works of art.

Aesthetic Perception

Seeing Like an Artist Look down a hallway. Compare the size of a nearby object to one that is farther away. How does the size of these objects appear to change as you walk down the hallway?

Using Linear Perspective

 Perspective is the method used to create the illusion of depth on a flat surface. Artists use one-point perspective to make viewers think they are looking at an object that is farther back than the rest of the image.

 Linear perspective is one way of using lines to show distance and depth. In one-point perspective, all lines that move back into space meet at a single point.

The **horizon line** is the point at which the earth and the sky meet. The horizon line is always at the viewer's eye level.

The **vanishing point** is the point on the horizon line where all parallel receding lines meet.

Vanishing Point

Horizon Line

Practice

Practice seeing linear perspective.

1. Look down the length of the hallway. Point each index finger toward the lines where the ceiling meets the walls beside you.

2. While standing still, move your fingers along those lines until they are pointing to the end of the hall. Notice how your arms move together down to eye level.

3. Do this again, but this time point to the lines where the walls meet the floor. How did your arms move?

Think about how the student artist used linear perspective.

Creative Expression

How can you use one-point perspective to create depth? Draw a city street using linear perspective.

1. Think of a place you have read about or studied. Make several sketches of objects and two or three buildings you want in your scene.

2. Lightly draw a horizon line. Mark a point where the lines will meet. Draw at least four lines coming out from the vanishing point on the horizon line. Using these guide lines, draw the buildings first, then the objects. Make the objects touch the top and bottom of the guide lines.

3. Paint your drawing.

Art Criticism

Describe Describe the cityscape you created. What objects did you include?

Analyze How did you use linear perspective in your work?

Interpret What objects communicate the kind of scene you created? Give your work a title.

Decide How could you apply the technique of linear perspective to another drawing?

Shading

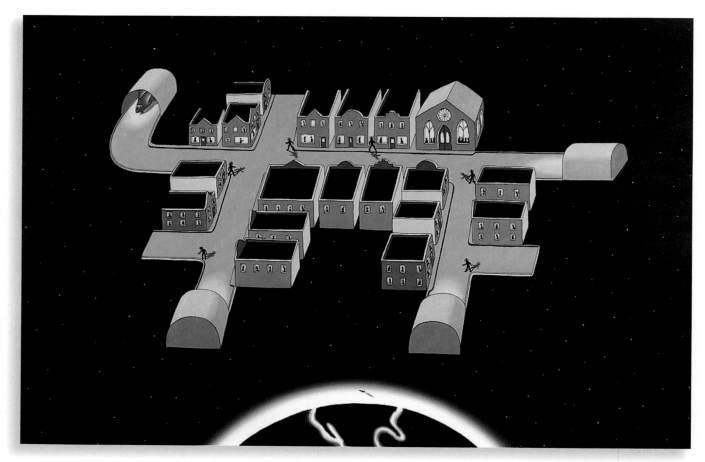

Look at the artwork on these pages. Notice the common theme and how the two artists created very different paintings by using space in their artwork. Both Robert McCall and Roger Brown used **shading** techniques to give these two-dimensional paintings the illusion of depth.

▲ **Roger Brown.** (American). *Homesick Proof Space Station.* 1987.
....
Oil on canvas. 48 × 72 inches
(121.92 × 182.88 cm.).
Phyllis Kind Gallery, Chicago, Illinois.

 Art History and Culture

How has American space travel influenced these artists and their artwork?

▲ **Robert McCall.** (American). *Space Station #1.* c. 1968.

Mixed media on canvas. 40½ × 53 inches (102.87 × 134.62 cm.). National Museum of Air and Space, Smithsonian Institution, Washington, D.C.

Study both works of art to find forms.

▶ Find a cylinder or cube. Are there overlapping forms?

▶ Identify the shading in these works of art.

▶ What effect does it have on the subject when an object's coloring goes from light to dark?

Aesthetic Perception

Seeing Like an Artist Look around the classroom. Can you tell what objects are casting shadows? Would you know what the objects were if you could see only the shadows?

Using Shading

Shading is the use of dark values to create the illusion of form and texture. Shading techniques include **hatching, cross-hatching, blending,** and **stippling.**

To create the illusion of form on a two-dimensional surface, artists use shading techniques.

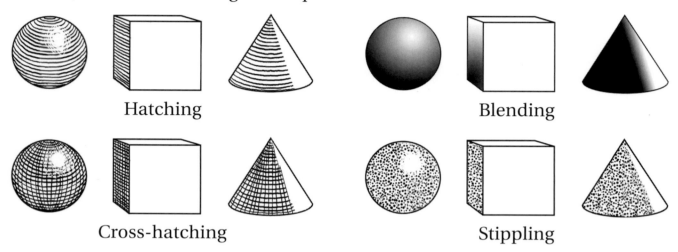

Hatching

Blending

Cross-hatching

Stippling

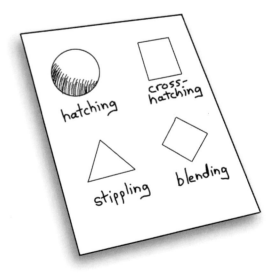

Practice

Create the illusion of forms by using different types of shading techniques. Use pencils.

1. Lightly draw four different shapes. Beneath each, write *hatching, cross-hatching, stippling,* or *blending.*

2. Make each shape appear to be a form by using the shading technique written below it.

◄ **Mike Kwon.**
Age 11.

Think about how the student artist used shading techniques to affect the appearance of the space station.

Creative Expression

What types of forms would you use to design a space station? Draw a three-dimensional space station. Use shading techniques to create the illusion of form.

1. Use simple shapes to sketch your space station. Use the shading techniques to change these shapes into forms.

2. Draw planets. Use blending techniques to move from light to dark. Try complementary colors for shading. Add white highlights.

3. Add an atmosphere by using the side of the oil pastel to make long sweeping marks.

Art Criticism

Describe Describe your space station and the shapes you used to draw it.

Analyze What shading techniques did you use?

Interpret How did the colors affect the appearance of your space station? Would you like to live there?

Decide If you drew another space station, what would you do differently?

# Form

Look at the artwork on these pages. Notice how Frank Stella and Tony Smith used three-dimensional forms to create interesting sculptures. Stella's piece is a *relief* sculpture because it hangs on the wall. Smith's is a *free-standing* piece because you can walk around it.

▲ **Frank Stella.** (American). *St. Michaels Counterguard.* 1984.
....
156 × 135 × 108 inches (396.24 × 342.9 × 274.32 cm.). Los Angeles County Museum of Art, Los Angeles, California.

 ## Art History and Culture

Smith's sculpture was inspired by a character in the book *Finnegan's Wake.* Stella's sculpture is his interpretation of Saint Michael's sword. The counterguard is the part of the sword designed to protect the inner hand and body in battle.

▲ **Tony Smith.** (American). *Gracehoper.* 1971.

Welded steel and paint 23 feet (7 meters). The Detroit Institute of Arts, Detroit, Michigan.

Study both works of art.

► Identify the forms, both geometric and free-form, that you see in each of the sculptures.

► What would be different about these works of art if the artists had decided to create them out of two-dimensional shapes instead of three-dimensional forms?

► Which artwork is a relief sculpture? Which is a free-standing sculpture?

Aesthetic Perception

Design Awareness Look around the classroom and find at least three shapes and three forms. Remember that shapes are two-dimensional, and forms have depth.

Using Form

In a work of art, **form** creates space. It allows you, the viewer, to see into the artwork.

Artists use paper-sculpture techniques to create three-dimensional forms from two-dimensional paper.

Scoring a straight line

 Hold a ruler in the center of a piece of paper. Run the point of the scissors along one edge of the ruler to cut the paper in a straight line.

Curling

 Hold one end of a long strip of paper. Grip the middle of the paper strip next to the side of a pencil. With a quick motion, pull the strip firmly across the pencil.

Scoring a curve

 Gradually press a bending curve with the point of the scissors.

Fringing

 Make parallel straight cuts along the edge of a piece of paper to create a ruffled look.

Pleating

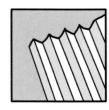 Fold a piece of paper in from the edge. Then fold the same amount of paper in the other direction. Continue folding back and forth in this manner.

Tab and slot

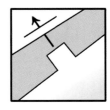 Tab and slot is a joining technique in which you cut a slot in one surface and insert a tab that has been cut out of another surface. You can glue or tape the tab for a stronger hold.

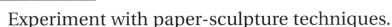
Practice

Experiment with paper-sculpture techniques.

1. Look at the paper-sculpture techniques on this page.
2. Using different kinds of paper, try each paper-sculpting technique.

◀ **Lauren Kaczynski.**
Age 10.

Think about how the student artist created a three-dimensional form from two-dimensional paper.

Creative Expression

How are forms created out of flat paper? Change a two-dimensional piece of paper into a three-dimensional form.

1. Use paper-sculpting techniques, especially scoring and folding to create forms. Use tab-and-slot techniques with glue to attach the pieces.

2. Cut into the paper without cutting it into two separate pieces.

3. Use markers to draw lines on the sculpture to enhance the edges of the forms.

4. Keep turning the sculpture and adding to the form so that it is interesting from many different points of view.

Art Criticism

Describe List the paper-sculpture techniques you used.

Analyze What types of forms did you create?

Interpret What mood does your artwork express?

Decide Were you successful in changing a two-dimensional piece of paper into a three-dimensional form?

Form in Architecture

▲ **Le Corbusier.** (Swiss).
Chapelle de Notre-Dame du Haut. 1950–1955.
....
Ronchamp, France.

Look at the artwork on these pages. Le Corbusier was an architect who designed *Chapelle de Notre-Dame du Haut* in France in 1950. The Sydney Opera House, in Sydney, Australia, was designed in 1957 by Jørn Utzon of Demark. Both architects used free-form, or organic forms found in nature, as a basis for their designs.

 Art History and Culture

How have these architects designed buildings that fit the surrounding culture?

▲ **Jørn Oberg Utzon.** (Danish). *Opera House.* 1957–1973
Sydney, Australia.

Study both works of art to find examples of use of form.

► What shapes and forms do you see in both structures?

► What is unique about these two buildings?

► Do you think both structures fit their environment? Why?

Aesthetic Perception

Design Awareness Look at the buildings in your environment. What objects in nature are similar to the forms in these buildings?

Using Form in Architecture

Architects design buildings, cities, and bridges using three-dimensional forms.

Shapes

Square

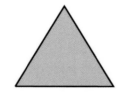
Triangle

Circle

Rectangle

Free-form

Forms

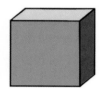
Cube

Cone

Sphere

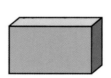
Rectangular solid

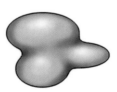
Free-form

Practice

Practice drawing some of the architectural forms you have learned about. Use pencil.

1. Lightly sketch the overall shape of a building or house you have seen.

2. Add forms from the examples above to your sketch. Keep the basic structure of your original drawing while adding new architectural features.

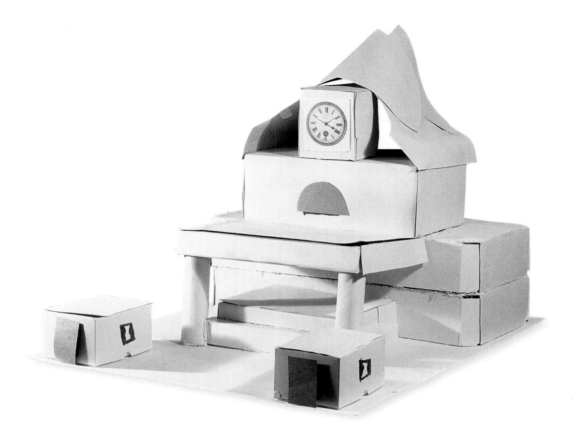

Think about the purpose of the student artist's public building.

Creative Expression

Use paper-sculpting techniques to create a uniquely formed public building.

1. Plan the building and its form. Consider what it will be used for.
2. Prepare the materials.
3. Put your building together.

Art Criticism

Describe Describe the unique building you have created.

Analyze Describe the various forms you used.

Interpret Does your building look like its function? Give it a name.

Decide Were you able to create the forms you had planned? Does the overall appearance of the building meet your expectations? What would you change?

Space, Shape, and Form

▲ **Marisol Escobar.** (Venezuelan).
The Family. 1962.
....
Painted wood and other found objects in three sections.
$82\frac{1}{2} \times 65\frac{1}{2} \times 15\frac{1}{2}$ inches (209.55 × 166.37 × 39.37 cm.).
Museum of Modern Art, New York, New York.

Art Criticism   Critical Thinking

Describe **What do you see?**

During this step you will collect information about the subject of the work.

▶ What does the credit line tell you about this work of art?

▶ Describe the people. What they are wearing? What they are doing?

Analyze **How is this work organized?**

Think about how the artist has used the elements and principles of art.

▶ Where do you see positive and negative shapes and forms in this work?

▶ Where did the artist use shading in this work?

▶ Which of the images of people are flat shapes? Which of the images of people are a combination of shapes and forms?

▶ Where do you see geometric and free-form shapes and forms?

Interpret **What is the artist trying to say?**

Use the clues you discovered during your analysis to find the message the artist is trying to give.

▶ Why are some parts two dimensional and some parts three dimensional?

▶ Explain the relationships of these people as you imagine they might be.

▶ Write a description of a day in the life of this family.

Decide **What do you think about the work?**

Use all the information you have gathered to decide whether this is a successful work of art.

▶ Is the work successful because it is realistic, because it is well organized, or because it has a strong message?

Space, Shape, and Form, continued

Show What You Know

Answer these questions on a separate sheet of paper.

1 _____ is the empty space that surrounds objects, shapes, and forms.
   A. Positive space
   B. Negative space
   C. Overlapping

2 Parallel lines that seem to move toward the same point as they move farther away from the viewer are known as _____.
   A. converging lines
   B. horizon lines
   C. scoring a straight line

3 One way of using lines to show distance and depth is by using _____.
   A. shape reversal
   B. curling
   C. linear perspective

4 _____ is a technique used for darkening values by adding black or darkening an area by repeating several lines close together.
   A. Fringing
   B. Architecture
   C. Shading

5 An _____ plans and designs building, cities, and bridges.
   A. archaeologist
   B. architect
   C. architecture

CAREERS IN ART
Architecture

Look around your neighborhood. Notice the public buildings, parks, and open areas.

Urban Design Architects design buildings, public spaces, and entire urban neighborhoods to accommodate people and their culture. Some restore buildings so that they are safe, attractive, and appear as they did when they were originally built.

Interior Design Interior designers plan the space inside homes, public buildings, businesses, or institutions. They consider color, space, shape, balance, building codes, and laws, as well as provisions for any special needs of the people that will use that space.

Marine Architects Marine architects plan, design, and oversee the building and the repairing of boats and ships.

▲ **Architect**

Space, Shape, and Form in Song Writing

Paul Tracey's musical "Our Little Blue Planet" features songs and stories that emphasize the importance of caring for Earth. Wherever we live on the planet, our actions affect people living elsewhere. One of his lyrics says "Our Little Blue Planet, our home out in space, without your environment, no human race." In his song "Save the Forest," Paul Tracey identifies a variety of trees from around the world. He researched them to point out their unique features in his lyrics. Here's an example:

▶ "Australia's got the *Gum* tree, koalas love to chew. In every English church yard, you'll always find a *Yew.*

▶ Zambia's got the *Babobab,* they say it's upside down. Its branches look like crooked roots high above the ground."

What to Do Research a specific tree and identify a feature that makes it unique.

1. Research a tree that interests you and identify its unique features. Describe its shape and form.

2. Write a rhyming couplet that includes the name of the tree and something special about it.

3. Share your line with a partner or group.

4. Combine lines and make a longer poem about trees.

▲ Paul Tracey. "Little Blue Planet."

 **Art Criticism**

Describe Did you describe the shape or form of the tree?

Analyze What did you think about as you prepared to write the couplet about this tree?

Interpret How do you feel about this tree now that you have researched it and written about it?

Decide How well did you describe this tree in poetry or lyrics?

Color and Pattern

◀ **Lavinia Fontana.** (Italian).
Portrait of a Noblewoman. c. 1600
. . . .
Oil on canvas. $45\frac{1}{4} \times 35\frac{1}{4}$ inches
(114.3 × 88.8 cm.). National Museum
of Women in the Arts, Washington, D.C.

Many artists use color and patterns to create interest, mood, and perspective in their drawings, paintings, prints, and sculptures.

Lavinia Fontana used warm colors and detailed patterns to create a realistic portrayal of her model in *Portrait of a Noblewoman.*

Artists use **color** to express a mood or feeling in their artwork.

▶ What colors do you see in this painting?

▶ Lavinia Fontana is noted for her attention to detail in her paintings. How does Fontana's use of color help make this portrait look realistic?

Artists use **pattern** to create designs that decorate the surfaces of fabrics and objects.

▶ What patterns do you see in this painting?

▶ Does this pattern remind you of the design you have seen on any other surface?

In This Unit you will learn and practice techniques using colors and pattern to add interest and feeling in your artwork.

Here are the topics you will study:
▶ Monochromatic colors
▶ Analogous colors
▶ Complementary colors
▶ Warm colors
▶ Cool colors
▶ Pattern

Lavinia Fontana
(1552–1614)

Lavinia Fontana was born in Bologna, Italy, in 1552. Her father, Prospero Fontana, taught her how to paint. Though it was difficult to be recognized as a female artist at that time, the city of Bologna was a great place for women to live because women's rights were recognized there more than in other places. Lavinia Fontana is considered the first female painter to have a successful career as an artist. She and her husband, Zappi, had eleven children. Zappi stayed home and took care of the family while Lavinia painted. Fontana's most notable works of art were religious and mythological paintings, in addition to her many portraits of Bolognese noblewomen. Only thirty-two of her signed and dated works exist today.

Monochromatic Colors

Look at these two works of art and notice the common hues that are repeated throughout. *King Family* is a drawing created by Ben Jones. His work shows the faces of familiar people, like the Dr. Martin Luther King, Jr., family. Jasper Johns created his collage and wax-based painting *Map,* and based it on the map of the United States. Johns's style emphasizes media rather than subject matter. Notice how both artists use color to unify their work.

◄ **Ben Jones.** (American). *King Family.* 1971.
. . . .
Gouache. 40 × 30 inches (101.6 × 76.2 cm.). Collection of the Studio Museum, Harlem, New York.

 Art History and Culture

How do the themes in these works of art honor American history?

▲ **Jasper Johns.** (American).
Map. 1962.

Encaustic and collage on canvas.
60 × 93 inches (152.4 × 236.22 cm.).
The Museum of Contemporary Art,
Los Angeles, California.

Study the monochromatic color schemes in both pieces of artwork.

▶ What one color is used most often in each work of art?

▶ Where do you see colors that are lighter or darker than the main color?

▶ What type of lines and shapes do you see in each work of art?

▶ What feeling is expressed in each artwork? How did these artists create these feelings?

Aesthetic Perception

Seeing Like an Artist What natural objects are made up of many variations of just one color?

Using Monochromatic Colors

Monochromatic means "one color." A color scheme that is monochromatic uses only one color and the tints and shades of that color.

Hue is another name for color. Red, blue, and yellow are **primary hues.** By mixing primary hues, you create **secondary hues.** Red and blue make violet. Red and yellow make orange. Blue and yellow make green.

Tint is a light value of a hue made by adding white.

Shade is a dark value of a hue made by adding black.

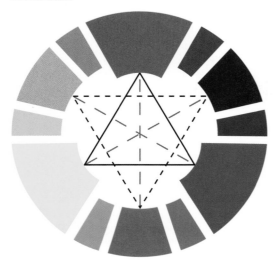

A **color wheel** is the spectrum bent into a circle.

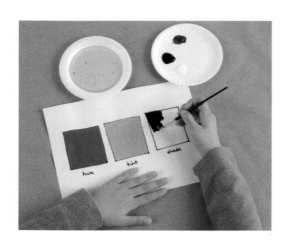

Practice

Practice mixing monochromatic tints and shades of a hue. Use tempera paint.

1. Draw three squares. Label the first *Hue,* the second *Tint,* and the third *Shade.*
2. Choose a hue for the first square.
3. Create a tint for the second square and a shade for the third square.
4. Paint each square.
5. Experiment to create various values of the primary hue.

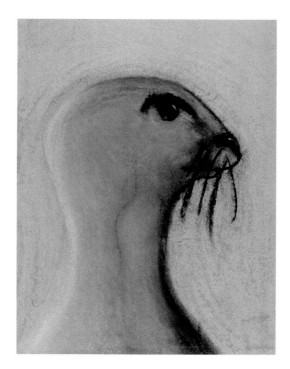

◀ **Paul Scott.**
Age 8.

Think about how the monochromatic color scheme affects the mood of the artwork.

 Creative Expression

What color dominates your favorite real or imaginary animal? Draw a real or imaginary animal. Use tints and shades of one hue. Use pastels on construction paper.

1. From your Art Journal, choose your favorite sketch of a real or imaginary animal.

2. Draw the animal large, so it fills the entire sheet of construction paper.

3. Color your animal. Use a hue, tints, and shades of that hue, and black and white pastels.

 **Art Criticism**

Describe Describe your animal. Is it real or imaginary?

Analyze What hue did you choose? Do your tints and shades vary a lot, or are they close to the original hue?

Interpret What mood did you create with the hues that you used?

Decide Were you successful in drawing an animal, using a monochromatic color scheme?

Analogous Colors

Look at these two works of art and notice how both the painting and the blanket use related colors to bring various shapes and lines together. Georgia O'Keeffe was interested in painting things that were uniquely American. She used colors found in the New Mexico desert. *Eye Dazzler* is a Navajo blanket. The Navajo of New Mexico are noted for their intricate weavings.

◀ **Georgia O'Keeffe.** (American).
Red and Pink Rocks and Teeth. 1938.
....
Oil on canvas. 21 × 13 inches (53.5 × 33 cm.).
The Art Institute of Chicago, Chicago, Illinois.

 Art History and Culture

What feeling from America's West have these artists reflected in their works of art?

Study both works of art to find analogous colors.

▶ Find the red colors in the painting and in the blanket.

▶ What orange areas or lines do you see in each work?

▶ What shapes do you see in both works of art?

▶ Find areas in both pieces that are lighter or darker than red.

 Artist unknown. (Navajo Tribe).
Navajo Blanket Eye Dazzler. 1890.

Wool, cotton, tapestry weave, slit tapestry, dovetailed tapestry. 75 × 57 inches (190.5 × 144 78 cm.). Dallas Museum of Art, Dallas, Texas.

Aesthetic Perception

Design Awareness Notice the colors used to paint your classroom and other parts of the school. Were analogous colors used? What mood is created with this choice of color scheme?

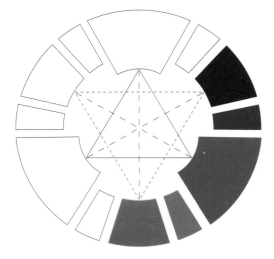

Using Analogous Colors

On the color wheel, **analogous colors** are located next to each other. They share a common color, or hue. For example, violet, blue, blue-green, and green are analogous colors. They share the color blue and are next to each other on the color wheel.

A **color scheme** is a plan for organizing colors. Analogous colors are one type of color scheme. The color scheme on the upper left shares the color blue. The color scheme on the lower left shares the color red.

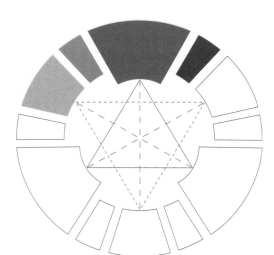

Intermediate hues are made by mixing a primary hue with an adjacent secondary hue. Red and orange make the intermediate color red-orange.

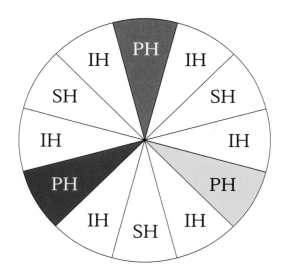

PH–Primary hue

SH–Secondary hue

IH–Intermediate hue

Create a color wheel. Use the primary, secondary, and intermediate colors. Use paint.

1. Fold a paper plate into twelve equal sections. Paint every fourth wedge a primary hue.

2. Combine neighboring primary hues to make secondary hues. Paint the three middle wedges with secondary hues.

3. Mix secondary hues with the primary hues to create intermediate hues. Paint the intermediate hues in the empty wedges between the secondary and primary hues to complete the color wheel.

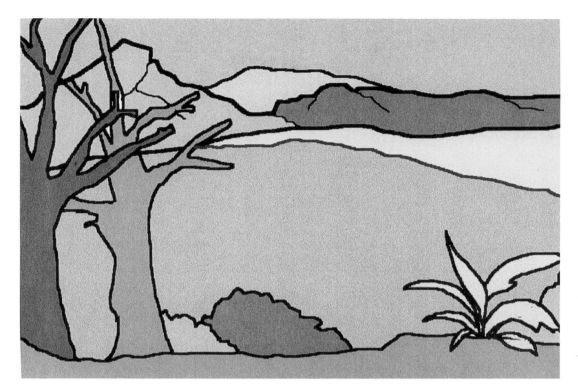

◄ **Mariella Lopez.**
Age 11.

Think about how the student artist used analogous colors to create a landscape painting.

 **Creative Expression**

How could you create a landscape painting using a computer? Use a paint program to create an analogous landscape.

1. Use the pencil tool in a paint program to create a landscape that includes a foreground, middleground, and background.

2. Check the colors in the palette for analogous color schemes.

3. Use brush, airbrush, and fill tools to paint the landscape.

Art Criticism

Describe What objects and shapes did you include in your landscape painting?

Analyze Name the analogous colors you used in your painting.

Interpret Where might you find a landscape that looks like this painting?

Decide Did you successfully use analogous colors to create a landscape painting?

Lesson 3 Complementary Colors

▲ **Artist unknown.** (Peru).
Featherwork Neckpiece. c. 1350–1476.
. . . .
Cotton, feathers, beads. Late Intermediate Period:
China style. 13¼ × 11½ inches (33.02 × 29.21 cm.).
Dallas Museum of Art, Dallas, Texas.

Look at the two pieces of artwork. Notice how the artists chose contrasting colors. *Featherwork Neckpiece* is an example of an adornment. An adornment decorates or adds beauty to an object or a person. Willis "Bing" Davis uses historical African patterns and forms as inspiration for his contemporary images. In Davis's work, he reflects on the images and feelings he experienced while attending a ritual dance in Nigeria.

 ## Art History and Culture

How have these artists honored cultural traditions through their artwork?

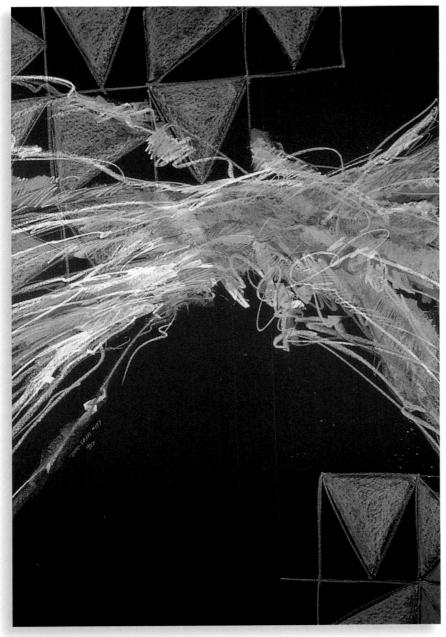

Study both works of art to find their complementary color schemes.

► What colors do you see?

► Do you see different shades or tints of these colors?

► What colors do you see repeated?

► Think about how the artist created contrast in each artwork.

 Willis "Bing" Davis. (American).
Ancestral Spirit Dance #187.
....
Oil pastel. 60 × 40 inches (152.4 × 101.6 cm.).
Private collection.

Aesthetic Perception

Design Awareness Do you notice any colors on your notebooks, bags, clothes, or other objects that contrast or look bright next to each other? Which colors do you notice?

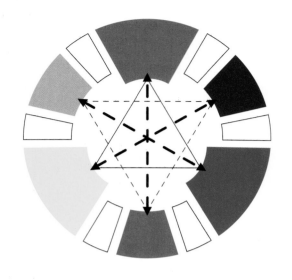

Using Complementary Colors

Colors opposite each other on the color wheel are called **complementary colors.** A complement of a color is the strongest contrast to the color. Complementary colors stand out when they are next to each other. Red and green, blue and orange, and violet and yellow are all pairs of complementary colors.

Complementary colors seem to vibrate when they are placed next to each other.

Mixing a color with its complement lowers the brightness of that color. When two complementary colors are mixed, the color becomes dull. Look at the intensity scale. The more orange that you add to the color blue, the darker it becomes.

Practice

Experiment with pieces of colored paper to see how complementary colors affect each other.

1. Choose two pieces of paper of complementary colors.

2. Cut a hole in one of the pieces of paper. Place the paper with the hole over the complementary-colored piece.

3. Notice how the complementary colors contrast.

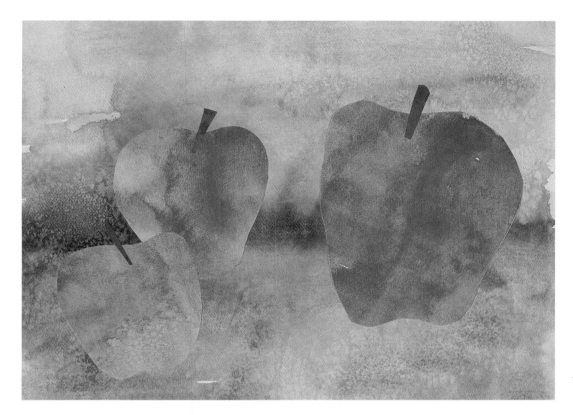

◀ **Patricia Lazzari.**
Age 10.

Think about the complementary colors that the student artist chose to use in this still life.

Creative Expression

How could you use complementary colors to make an exciting still life? Design and create a still-life painting with watercolors.

1. Select fruit of like colors.
2. Refer to the sketches in your Art Journal, and draw the fruit. Use different sizes and shapes on squares of paper.
3. Paint the fruit with shades and tints of one chosen hue.
4. Cut out the fruit shapes.
5. Arrange and glue the fruit on a complementary-colored background.

Art Criticism

Describe What objects did you include in your still life?

Analyze Which complementary colors did you use in this still life?

Interpret How do your complementary colors create contrast and visual excitement?

Decide Do the complementary colors add excitement to your still-life watercolor?

Lesson 4 Warm and Cool Colors

▲ **Raoul Dufy.** (French). *Fenetre Ouverte Devant la Mer (Window Open to the Sea).* 1923.

Oil on canvas. 29 × 23 inches (73.66 × 58.42 cm.). New Orleans Museum of Art, New Orleans, Louisiana.

Look at the artwork on these pages. Identify how the warm and cool colors affect the mood of the artwork. Dufy used the contrast of warm and cool colors in *Window Open to the Sea* to show the difference between the warm interior scene and the cool ocean scene. Mabe used contrast between light and dark as well as warm and cool to express his emotions in his nonobjective painting *Melancholy Metropolis.*

 Art History and Culture

Which work of art is abstract? Which work of art is nonobjective?

◀ **Manabu Mabe.** (Brazilian). *Melancholy Metropolis.* 1961.

Oil on canvas. $72\frac{7}{8} \times 78\frac{7}{8} \times 1\frac{1}{4}$ inches (185.40 × 200.5 × 2.5 cm.). Walker Art Center, Minneapolis, Minnesota.

Study both paintings to find the warm and cool colors.

▶ What colors do you see that remind you of water or a cool winter day?

▶ What colors do you see that remind you of fire?

▶ Imagine these works of art painted in only cool colors. How would this change the mood of these paintings?

▶ Imagine these works of art painted in only warm colors. How would this change the mood of these paintings?

▶ Why do you think these artists decided to use both warm and cool colors in these paintings?

Aesthetic Perception

Design Awareness Take time to notice how cool and warm colors are used in your school, home, and other indoor areas.

Using Warm and Cool Colors

Sometimes colors are divided into warm and cool colors. They make us think about warm and cool things when we see them.

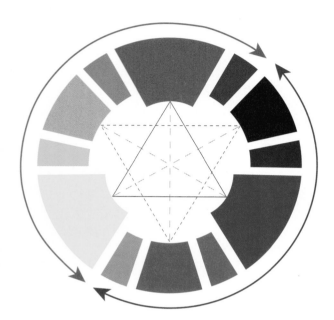

Warm colors are red, orange, and yellow. They suggest warmth and seem to move toward the viewer. They remind us of the colors of the sun or fire. Artists use warm colors to express a warm mood in their artwork.

Cool colors are blue, green, and violet. They suggest coolness and seem to move away from the viewer. Cool colors remind us of ice, water, and grass. Artists use cool colors to express a cool mood in their artwork.

Practice

Use tissue paper to experiment with warm and cool colors.

1. Cut out squares of colored tissue paper. Separate the warm colors and the cool colors.

2. Overlap warm-colored and cool-colored tissue paper. Then overlap the cool colors with each other. Do the same with the warm colors.

3. Notice how the colors change when they are placed together.

◀ **Ester Stewart Dage.**
Age 11.

Think about how the warm and cool colors contribute to the mood of the artwork.

🎨 Creative Expression

How can you create a specific mood in a collage? Use warm and cool colors to create a collage.

1. Think about the warm and cool colors you like.

2. Cut free-form and geometric shapes out of colored drawing paper and tissue paper.

3. Arrange your shapes on white paper. Combine the warm and cool colors. Allow the tissue-paper shapes to overlap some of the drawing-paper shapes.

4. Use a glue-water wash to attach your shapes onto the white background.

❗? Art Criticism

Describe What colors did you overlap? What shapes did you use?

Analyze Did you use warm and cool colors to organize your collage? Did changes occur when you overlapped colors with the tissue paper?

Interpret What mood was created with your use of colors?

Decide How would you change this collage?

Pattern

Look at the artwork on these pages and notice the patterns. Both *Half of a Tunic,* from the Wari culture of ancient Peru, and *Ceremonial Panel,* from the Kuba Group of twentieth century Congo, express aspects of each culture through the use of patterns on textiles.

◄ **Artist unknown** (Wari Culture, Peru). *Half of a Tunic.* 600–900 A.D.
. . . .
Plain weave sections tie-dyed and recombined, alpaca. 77 × 31 inches (195.58 × 78.74 cm.). Museum of International Folk Art, Santa Fe, New Mexico.

 Art History and Culture

These works of art were created during different periods of time and in different parts of the world. What similarities do you see in these works of art?

◀ **Artist unknown.** (Kuba Group, Western Kasai Province, Congo). *Ceremonial Panel.* 1950–1975.

Cut-pile and linear embroidery on plain-weave raffia palm. 22 × 23½ inches (55.88 × 59.69 cm.). Museum of International Folk Art, Santa Fe, New Mexico.

Study both weavings to find examples of patterns.

▶ Look at both works of art. Identify simple and complex geometric shapes that appear in the patterns.

▶ Find the types of lines that are used in the patterns in both textiles.

▶ What colors are used to create the patterns in these works of art?

▶ How are these two textiles similar? How are they different?

Aesthetic Perception

Seeing Like an Artist Look for interesting patterns on plants and animals. Share what you find with the class.

Using Pattern

A **pattern** is a repeated design that decorates the surface of fabrics and other objects.

A **motif** is the object that is repeated, or a unit of objects that is repeated, in a pattern.

In a **random pattern** the motif is repeated in no noticeable order.

Practice

Find patterns in wallpaper samples.

1. Look through the wallpaper samples provided.
2. Find patterns that use different combinations of lines, shapes, and colors.
3. Identify the motifs used in each pattern.

◀ **Callie Annett.**
Age 11.

Think about how the student artist created a motif to design an original pattern.

Creative Expression

How could you create a design for wrapping paper? Create a pattern using a motif.

1. Choose your favorite motif sketch and draw it on a foam printing plate.

2. Cut out the motif and add details by etching lines with a ballpoint pen.

3. Place some ink on the inking plate. Spread out the ink using a brayer.

4. Use the brayer to roll ink onto the foam printing plate.

5. Fill the paper with a random arrangement of prints.

6. When dry, use oil pastels to add details.

Art Criticism

Describe What motif did you use to create the pattern on your wrapping paper?

Analyze Did you create a random pattern on your wrapping-paper design?

Interpret What type of gift would you wrap with this paper?

Decide How could you use this wrapping-paper to teach someone about using a motif to create a random pattern?

Decorative Pattern

Look at the artwork on these pages. Notice how the designers used patterns to decorate the surfaces. The motif on the Kongo bowl has a random pattern created by the staining process. Louis Sullivan's *Elevator Grill* has alternating patterns throughout the design.

▲ **Artist unknown.** (Kongo peoples, Congo and Democratic Republic of the Congo). *Bowl.* Late-nineteenth to early-twentieth century.
....
Ceramic and resin. $5\frac{7}{8} \times 4\frac{1}{8} \times 5\frac{7}{8}$ inches (14.9 × 10.49 × 14.94 cm.). National Museum of African Art, Smithsonian Institution, Washington, D.C.

 Art History and Culture

How have these artists incorporated art elements into the design of objects that will be used by their community?

Study both pieces to find decorative patterns.

▶ Look at both pieces of art and identify the motifs used to create patterns.

▶ What types of lines and shapes are the motifs in the Kongo *Bowl*?

▶ What types of lines and shapes are used to create motifs on the *Elevator Grill*?

▶ Louis Sullivan created art that was functional as well as beautiful. What function would this iron design serve in an elevator door?

▶ Both designers thought about nature when creating their decorative patterns. What natural objects can you think of that look like these works of art?

◀ **Louis Sullivan.** (American).
Elevator Grill. 1893–1894.
. . . .
Bronze-plated cast iron. 73 × 31 inches (185.42 × 78.74 cm.). High Museum of Art, Atlanta, Georgia.

Aesthetic Perception

Design Awareness Look at the surface designs of the objects you use today. Identify the types of patterns you see. Does the pattern help with the function of the object, or is it just decoration?

Using a Decorative Pattern

A **regular pattern** occurs when a motif is repeated with the same amount of space between each motif.

An **alternating pattern** repeats motifs but changes positions of the motif or adds a second motif to the pattern.

A **random pattern** occurs when the motif is repeated in no apparent order.

Practice

Design regular and alternating patterns using geometric shapes. Use a pencil.

1. Fold your paper in half. Label one side *regular pattern* and the other side *alternating pattern*.

2. Draw a geometric shape and repeat it to create a regular pattern.

3. To create an alternating pattern on the other side of the paper, add a second geometric shape to the shape you used in the regular pattern.

Think about how the student artist used a decorative pattern to add interest to the clay bowl.

Creative Expression

How could you design a clay coil bowl? Create a motif to decorate the surface of the bowl.

1. Make a small clay ball, and press it flat to make the base of your bowl.

2. Using a flat hand, roll pieces of clay in one direction into coils. Stack the coils on top of one another to make the walls of the bowl. Smooth out the inside coils to join them all together.

3. Make small clay shapes for the motif of your pattern.

4. Attach the motifs to the outside coils using slip and scoring techniques.

5. Scratch lines in the clay to enhance the pattern.

Art Criticism

Describe What is the theme of your clay coil bowl?

Analyze How does this type of pattern work for the motif you used?

Interpret What does this artwork say about you?

Decide If you were to make a set of bowls, would you make them all the same or would you vary the motifs or the pattern within the same theme?

Color and Pattern

▲ **Paul Cézanne.** (French).
Pierrot and Harlequin. 1888.

Oil on canvas. $42\frac{1}{2} \times 31\frac{7}{8}$ inches (107.95 × 80.95 cm.).
State Puskin Museum, Moscow, Russia.

⚠️ Art Criticism Critical Thinking

Describe **What do you see?**

During this step you will collect information about the subject of the work.

▶ What does the credit line tell you about the painting?

▶ Describe the people. What they are wearing? What they are doing?

▶ What do you see in the background?

Analyze **How is this work organized?**

Think about how the artist has used the elements and principles of art.

▶ What complementary colors do you see?

▶ Which warm colors and which cool colors do you see?

▶ Where do you see patterns?

Interpret **What is the artist trying to say?**

Use the clues you discovered during your analysis to find the message the artist is trying to show.

▶ How do the colors affect the mood of this painting?

▶ What kind of act do these men perform? Write a paragraph describing the act from the time the curtain opens until it closes.

Decide **What do you think about the work?**

Use all the information you have gathered to decide whether this is a successful work of art.

▶ Is the work successful because it is realistic, because it is well organized, or because it has a strong message?

Show What You Know

Answer these questions on a separate sheet of paper.

1 _____ means "one color."
  A. Analogous
  B. Monochromatic
  C. Primary

2 _____ colors are next to each other on the color wheel.
  A. Complementary
  B. Secondary
  C. Analogous

3 _____ colors are across from each other on the color wheel.
  A. Monochromatic
  B. Warm
  C. Complementary

4 _____ colors are blue, green, and violet. They seem to move away from the viewer.
  A. Cool
  B. Warm
  C. Motif

5 A repeated design that decorates the surface of a fabric or other object is a _____.
  A. hue
  B. pattern
  C. shape

LEARNING ABOUT MUSEUMS

The Metropolitan Museum of Art

The Metropolitan Museum of Art in New York City is one of the world's largest museums. It has more than two million works of art, spanning 5,000 years of culture. The museum was founded in 1870 and is located in Central Park. Its Egyptian collection is second only to the one in Cairo, Egypt. Major collections in the museum, in addition to the paintings, include arms and armor, Chinese art, costumes, musical instruments, primitive art, French and American furniture, and photographs. More than 4.5 million people from around the world visit the Metropolitan Museum of Art each year.

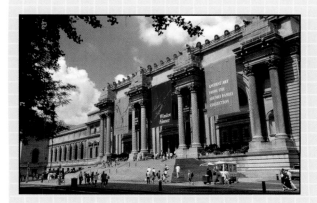

Color and Pattern in Theatre

"On the Day You Were Born" is a play based on a book by Debra Frasier. It describes events in nature on the day a child is born. The artists and actors use visual and rhythmic patterns with puppets, paintings, poems, and music to portray these natural events.

Here is a part of the text from "On the Day You Were Born."

"On the day you were born
the Earth turned, the Moon pulled,
the Sun flared, and, then, with a push,
you slipped out of the dark quiet
where suddenly you could hear…
a circle of people singing
with voices familiar and clear."

What to Do Use your body and voice to express information about science and nature.

1. List some natural events (falling tides, moving air, exploding volcanoes, and pulling gravity) to express through movement.

2. In small groups, create regular, random, or alternating patterns of movement to represent these events.

3. Think of one to three ways to interpret your natural event. Use interesting vocal sounds to accompany your movement ideas. Find a shape or design for the group to hold for the ending of the performance.

4. Perform your natural-event dance for the class.

▲ In the Heart of the Beast Theater. "On the Day You Were Born."

 Art Criticism

Describe Describe the way your group interpreted your natural event.

Analyze Explain why you chose specific patterns of movement or sound to express the event.

Interpret What did you learn about your natural event by interpreting it through movement and sound?

Decide Were you successful in using sound, rhythm, and movement in your dance?

Proportion and Distortion

Proportion and distortion are used by artists in both sculptural forms and in pictures.

Although this statue is much larger than most human beings, the artist used normal body proportions to create it. One body part does not look unusual or out of place when compared to the other parts.

◀ **Viola Frey.** (American).
Grandmother Series: July Cone Hat. 1982.

Glazed earthenware. $86\frac{1}{2} \times 21 \times 18$ inches
(219.71 $\times$ 53.34 $\times$ 45.72 cm.). The Nelson-Atkins
Museum of Art, Kansas City, Missouri.

Artists use several techniques to create **proportion** in a work of art.

▶ Does Viola Frey's *July Cone Hat* look like a living person?

▶ How did Viola Frey use clothing to increase size? What effect do the shoes and hat have on the statue?

▶ How would the statue look different if there was a living person standing next to it?

Distortion is used by artists in paintings, drawings, and sculpture to express feelings and ideas.

▶ Look at the dimensions of this statue. Is the height accurate for a typical grandmother?

In This Unit you will learn about and practice techniques of proportion and distortion to add interest and feeling in your artwork. Here are the topics you will study:
▶ Body proportion
▶ Realistic scale
▶ Unrealistic scale
▶ Face and profile proportions
▶ Distortion
▶ Ratio and scale

Viola Frey
(1933–)

Viola Frey grew up in the small town of Lodi, California. There was not much to do in such a small town, so she entertained herself by observing people. She studied art in high school and went on to study both painting and ceramics. Later, she taught art at the California College of Arts and Crafts. Her large statues of people are made from clay that has to be cut into many pieces, fired, and then put back together. She uses an electric lift to work on the taller parts of these sculptures. Many of her sculptures are very large and colorful, and are dressed in modern clothing. Frey describes her work as *organic* because it projects such a strong feeling of life and personality.

Proportion

▲ **John Steuart Curry.** (American).
Tornado Over Kansas. 1929.
....
Oil on canvas. $46\frac{1}{4} \times 60\frac{3}{8}$ inches
(117.48 × 153.34 cm.). Muskegon Museum of
Art, Muskegon, Michigan.

Look at these two works of art. Notice how the
two artists used accurate proportions to represent
people realistically in different situations. The
people in *Bird Watchers* are calm and standing
vertically. The people in *Tornado Over Kansas* are
active and moving diagonally.

 Art History and Culture

Curry was a member of a group of artists known as American
Regionalists. They painted the scenes and events of their sections
of the United States.

▲ **George Tooker.** (American). *Bird Watchers.* 1948.

Egg tempera on gesso board. $26\frac{3}{4} \times 32\frac{1}{4}$ inches (67.95 × 81.92 cm.). New Britain Museum of Art, New Britain, Connecticut.

Study both works of art to identify the use of proportion.

▶ Look at the man's arm in *Tornado Over Kansas* and imagine it on one of the children. How would this affect the looks of the child?

▶ What does the size of the people in *Tornado Over Kansas* suggest about them?

▶ What clues do you see in each of the paintings that tell you how tall the people are?

▶ Do the people in *Bird Watchers* look shorter than average adults?

Aesthetic Perception

Design Awareness Study cartoon characters and notice how many of them are drawn with exaggerated proportions. Think about why they are drawn this way.

Using Proportion

Proportion is the principle of art related to the size relationships of one part to another, such as a hand to a wrist. Artists use several techniques to draw things in proportion.

Although people vary in size and shape, most people have the same body proportions.

Artists use the length of the head, from the chin to the top of the skull, to help them in measuring proportion. The average adult is seven and one-half heads tall. A child may be five heads tall, while an infant might be only three heads tall.

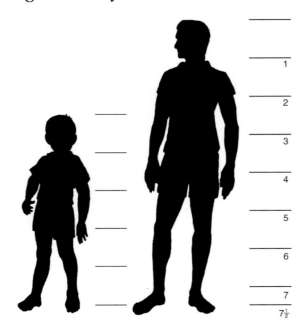

Practice

Estimate body proportions. Use string.

1. With a string, measure a partner's head from the top of the skull to the bottom of the chin. Using the length of the head as a unit of measurement, measure the rest of your partner's body. For example, the length of the arm might be two head lengths.

2. Record and compare your findings with those of your partner.

◀ **Andrew Williams.**
Age 11.

Think about the proportion this student artist used.

 Creative Expression

How can you use the sighting technique to draw a person in proportion? Sketch a model. Use the sighting technique to determine proportion.

1. Think about proportion as it relates to people. Use the sighting technique to determine the proportion of your model.

2. Use chalk and a soft eraser to lightly sketch your model.

3. Add color to your drawing by covering over all the chalk lines with oil pastels.

 **Art Criticism**

Describe Explain the steps you followed as you used the sighting technique.

Analyze How many heads tall is your figure?

Interpret What mood does your drawing convey?

Decide Were you able to successfully use the sighting technique to draw the model in proportion?

Look at these works of art and notice how scale is used to show the differences in size between the adults and the children in the paintings.

◄ **Domenico Ghirlandaio.**
(Italian). *Francesco Sasetti and His Son Teodoro.* c. 1480.

Tempera on wood. $29\frac{1}{2} \times 20\frac{1}{2}$ inches (74.93 × 52.07 cm.). The Metropolitan Museum of Art, New York, New York.

 Art History and Culture

Emperor Shah Jahan had the Taj Mahal built as a tomb for his wife.

Study both paintings to learn about scale.

▶ How big are the people in each work of art?

▶ What objects give the viewer clues to help judge the sizes of the man and his son in Nanha's painting?

▶ Do both children seem to be in realistic proportion and scale to the adults they appear next to?

▶ As a viewer, where are you in relation to each painting? How does this affect the way you see the people in these paintings?

▲ **Nanha.** (Indian). *Emperor Shah Jahan and His Son, Suja.* 1625–1630.

Colors on gilt on paper. $15\frac{5}{6} \times 10\frac{5}{16}$ inches (40.21 × 102.39 cm.). Metropolitan Museum of Art, New York, New York.

Aesthetic Perception

Seeing Like an Artist Compare the size of the objects in the lower-grade classrooms in your school with the size of the objects in the upper-grade classrooms.

Using Scale

Scale is similar to proportion in that it relates to size relationships. The difference is that scale refers to size as measured against a standard reference, such as the human body. A scale can be realistic or unrealistic.

Realistic Scale When an artist creates a work of art in which everything seems to fit together and make sense in size relationships, the scale is called *realistic*.

Unrealistic Scale When an artist creates size relationships that do not make sense, the scale becomes *unrealistic*.

Practice

Use a realistic scale when drawing an object. Use pencil.

1. Draw your hand to create an object of standard size.

2. Select an object that is either larger or smaller than your hand. Draw the object in realistic scale to your hand. The entire object does not have to fit on your paper.

◀ **Marcia Saunders.**
Age 10.

Think about how the student artist used both realistic and unrealistic scale in this collage.

 Creative Expression

How can you use unrealistic scale to emphasize an object in your artwork? Create a collage. Use unrealistic scale.

1. Think about an indoor or outdoor background to use in your collage and the objects that you will add. Cut out pictures of objects, some that are in proper scale and one or two that are too large or too small for the other objects.

2. Arrange your collected images so that they overlap and touch the edges of your paper. Keep the arrangement organized so that it is almost realistic.

3. Glue down the background. Next, glue the remaining objects. Make sure that at least one object shows unrealistic scale.

 **Art Criticism**

Describe Describe the objects you selected for your collage.

Analyze How are the objects arranged to create unrealistic scale?

Interpret What emotion does your collage convey?

Decide Do you feel you were able to clearly portray unrealistic scale in an organized way?

Face Proportions

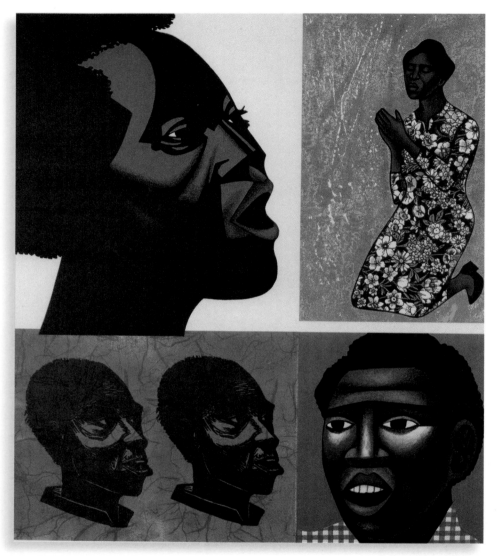

Look at these works of art and notice the similar placement of the eyes in the faces.

▲ **Elizabeth Catlett.** (American). *Singing Their Songs*. 1992. From *For My People*.

Color lithograph on paper. $15\frac{3}{4} \times 13\frac{3}{4}$ inches (40.01 × 34.93 cm.). National Museum of Women in the Arts, Washington, D.C.

 Art History and Culture

Robert Henri founded a group of eight artists called "The Eight." They chose to paint everyday life as they saw it in the city. They were nicknamed the "Ashcan School."

▲ **Robert Henri.** (American).
Tilly. 1917.
....
Oil on canvas. 24 × 20 inches
(60.96 × 50.8 cm.). Lowe Art
Museum, Coral Gables, Florida.

Study both paintings to investigate face proportions.

► What changes and what stays the same in the positions of the faces in these works of art?

► How is a mouth drawn differently in a side profile view as compared to the way it is drawn in a front view?

► Where are the ears in relation to the eyes and nose? Is this true for all faces in these works of art?

► How do the child's features compare to the adult's features?

► How are the characters in these works of art communicating?

Aesthetic Perception

Seeing Like an Artist Look at people's faces that you see throughout the day. Notice the placement of each feature and think about how you would correctly draw the features.

Using Face Proportions

Artists use **face proportions** to correctly draw features on human faces. Lightly drawn lines are **guide lines** used by artists to create both full-face and profile portraits more accurately.

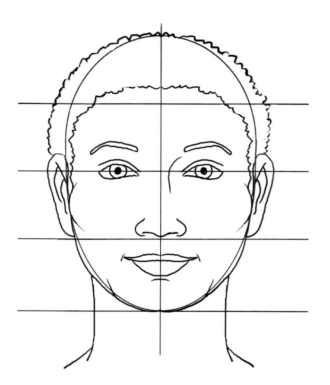

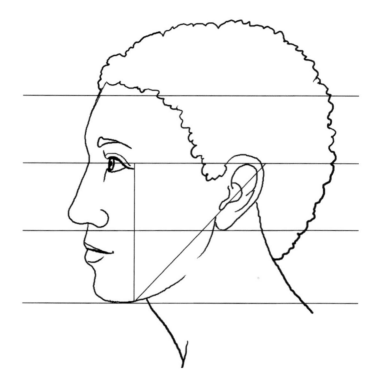

Practice

Practice drawing a profile. Use pencil.

1. Draw the shape of the head in profile. Add guide lines. Use the second drawing shown above as a reference.

2. Add the eye, nose, mouth, chin, ear, hair, and neck.

◀ **Shelby Stephen.**
Age 10.

Think about how the student artist used face proportions to correctly draw a portrait.

🎨 Creative Expression

What is the best way to draw features on a portrait? Working with a partner, draw a portrait using face proportions.

1. Think about the shape and size of your partner's head.

2. Measure the size of your partner's head. Mark off the dimensions on paper. Next, lightly draw guide lines for the eyes. Keep proportion in mind.

3. Draw the hair, eyebrows, neck, shoulders and clothing.

4. Use watercolors to paint the portrait.

❗❓ Art Criticism

Describe List the steps you followed to measure and draw face proportions.

Analyze What measurements did you use to place the features on the head using accurate proportions?

Interpret What does the person in your portrait seem to be thinking?

Decide Were you successful in drawing the features of your portrait in proportion? What would you do to make it better?

Distortion of Body Proportions

Look at these two works of art, and notice how the artists distorted body proportions in the two women. Think about how this affects the mood of the paintings.

▲ **Fernando Botero.** (Colombian). *Ruben's Wife.* 1963.

Oil on canvas. $72\frac{1}{8} \times 70\frac{1}{8}$ inches (183.21 × 178.13 cm.). Solomon R. Guggenheim Museum, New York, New York.

 Art History and Culture

How have these artists communicated ideas about their culture through the use of distortion? Which subject seems wealthy and content? Which subject appears thin and weary?

Study both paintings to find examples of distortion of body proportions.

▶ Where do you see a lengthened or stretched figure? A figure that is enlarged?

▶ Why do you think the artists chose to distort the figures in these ways?

▶ What emotions do these figures suggest?

▶ How would the effects of these works of art be different if they were not distorted?

◀ **Amedeo Modigliani.** (Italian). *Portrait of a Polish Woman.* 1918.
....
Oil on canvas. $39\frac{1}{2} \times 25\frac{1}{2}$ inches (100.33 × 64.77 cm.). Philadelphia Museum of Art, Philadelphia, Pennsylvania.

Aesthetic Perception

Design Awareness Look at the comics section of a newspaper for examples of distortion of body proportions. What do you think was the reason for these uses of distortion?

Using Distortion of Body Proportions

Distortion is the bending or pulling of an object or figure out of its normal shape to communicate ideas or feelings.

Artists sometimes start with real body proportions and stretch, twist, shrink, or enlarge them to emphasize thoughts, feelings, and ideas.

From a newspaper, find examples of distortion in editorial cartoons.

1. Look through a newspaper for an editorial cartoon about a famous person. Next, find a photo of that same person.

2. Compare the distortion of the body proportions in the person in the cartoon with his or her features in the photo.

◀ **Kristen Patrick.**
Age 9.

Think about how the student artist used distortion of body proportions to create an original comic-strip superhero.

Creative Expression

What kind of character would you create if you were a cartoonist? Create an original comic-strip superhero using distortion of body proportions.

1. Think about comic-strip characters you are familiar with. Then make several sketches of your own original comic-strip superhero.

2. Choose one sketch. Distort one or more body features to show the superpower of your character. Give your character a name.

Art Criticism

Describe Describe the body feature you distorted on your character.

Analyze Explain how you decided which feature to distort and how you distorted that feature.

Interpret What mood is expressed by your character? Does your character seem to be silly, serious, angry, confused, or relaxed, or does your character express a different mood?

Decide Do you like the way the distortion of body proportions changed the mood of your drawing? Explain.

Distortion of Face Proportions

▲ **Charlie James.** (Southern Kwakiutl).
Sun Transformation Mask. Early
nineteenth century.
••••••••••••••••••••••••••••••••••••••
Royal British Columbia Museum, British Columbia, Canada.

▲ **Elon Webster.** (Iroquois).
False Face Mask. 1937.
••••••••••••••••••••••••••••••••••••••
Wood. Cranbrook Institute of Science, Bloomfield
Hills, Michigan.

Look at the artwork and identify the features of the
faces that are distorted. Notice how different areas of
the face can be stretched or changed to express an idea
or emotion.

 Art History and Culture

Masks were often used to represent cultural beliefs or emotions
in ceremonies. Look at these masks and identify the feelings
they communicate.

▲ **Artist unknown.** (Tlatilco Valley of Mexico). *Mask.* c. twelfth through nineteenth century B.C.
....
Ceramic pigment. $5\frac{1}{4}$ inches tall (13.33 cm.). The Metropolitan Museum of Art, New York, New York.

▲ **Artist unknown.** (Kwele). *Kwele Face Mask.* c. Nineteenth through twentieth century.
....
Wood and paint. $20\frac{3}{4}$ inches tall (52.71 cm.). The Metropolitan Museum of Art, New York, New York.

Study all four masks to identify the use of distortion.

▶ Which mask shows the most distortion? Which shows the least?

▶ Use one adjective to describe the expressive quality of each mask.

▶ What do you think was the purpose of each mask?

▶ What do all four masks have in common? How are they different?

Aesthetic Perception

Design Awareness Look closely for distortion used in advertisements. What are the distortions emphasizing, and why?

Using Distortion of Face Proportions

Distortion can be in the form of exaggeration. **Exaggeration** is making something bigger than it normally is.

Exaggeration is used by an artist to make a feature more exciting and expressive than it would be in realistic proportions.

Practice

Design a mask. Use pencil.

1. Design a mask that expresses your enthusiasm or celebration of something. Make sketches of your mask from different angles.

2. Distort facial features of the mask by using exaggeration to emphasize what you are enthusiastic about or what you are celebrating.

◄ **Emma Sams.**
Age 10.

Think about how the student artist used distortion of face proportions in her work of art.

Creative Expression

How does a mask express a certain emotion or idea? Create a papier-mâché mask. Use distortion in one or more of the features.

1. Tear one-inch strips of newspaper. Dip the strips into paste and squeeze off the excess liquid. Lay the strips over the outside of a plastic milk container. Overlap two layers of newspaper strips to make the base of your mask.

2. Allow the base to dry, then add the features. Distort the features. Apply two more layers of papier-mâché, and let the mask base dry overnight.

3. When it is dry, pop your mask off the container and trim the edges. Paint the mask and apply other objects.

Art Criticism

Describe List the steps you followed to create your mask.

Analyze How did you distort the features on your mask?

Interpret What emotions or ideas does your mask suggest? Which features communicate these emotions or ideas?

Decide Were you successful in creating a mask that has distorted features expressing a certain feeling or idea?

Scale and Proportion

Look at the sculptures and notice how the artists have used accurate proportions. Each artist has combined objects from the real world with his sculpture. The objects and figures fit together because they have the same scale.

◀ **George Segal.** (American).
Walk Don't Walk. 1976.
· ·
Plaster, cement, metal, painted wood, and electric light. 104 × 72 × 72 inches (264.16 × 182.88 × 182.88 cm.). Whitney Museum of American Art, New York, New York.

 Art History and Culture

Duane Hanson's lifelike sculptures have been made possible because of the invention of new materials. How do you think someone from the eighteenth century would react to one of his works of art?

Study both sculptures to identify realistic and lifelike objects.

▶ Which artist's work looks more realistic? Explain.

▶ What are the people doing in each sculpture?

▶ Why did the artists include real objects with their sculptures?

▶ Can you tell which objects in each work were not created by the sculptor, but were added?

▲ **Duane Hanson.** (American).
Football Player. 1981.

. . . .

Oil on polyvinyl. $43\frac{1}{4} \times 30 \times 31\frac{1}{2}$ inches
(109.86 × 76.2 × 80.01 cm.). Lowe Art Museum,
Miami, Florida.

Aesthetic Perception

Design Awareness If students in your school wanted to create sculptures to represent the school's people and activities, what would the sculptures look like?

Using Scale and Proportion

Body proportions are defined in ratios of one part of the body to another.

A **ratio** is a comparison of size between two things. Often, artists use the measurement of the head to the length of an adult body, which is about seven times the length of the head. Therefore, the ratio is 1 (head) to 7 (heads per body length) and is written 1:7.

Scale is similar to proportion in that it relates to size relationships. The difference is that scale refers to size as measured against something that is common, such as the human body.

Practice

Find examples of scale and proportion, using props.

1. With a small group of classmates, think of a scene that George Segal or Duane Hanson might create. Collect props that are either in scale or out of scale to your body proportions.

2. Set up your living sculpture for the class to see.

◀ **Fort Daniel Elementary fifth-grade class.**

Think about how the artists used scale and proportion to create a realistic-looking scene.

Creative Expression

What effect would a life-size sculpture have if you placed it somewhere in your school? Use scale and proportion to create a life-size soft sculpture. Place it in a real environment in your school.

1. Think about available items you have to make a life-size soft sculpture. Work in small groups. Plan and make sketches of your figure and of the environment.

2. Divide responsibilities. For example, some students can create a soft-sculpture head while others stuff clothes with newspaper. Others can construct the environment. Make sure your figure is in scale with the environment.

3. Make a sign that gives the title and the students' names who created the sculpture.

Art Criticism

Describe Describe the materials you used to create your sculpture and the environment.

Analyze Whom does your character represent? What is the setting of your sculpture?

Interpret What is the mood of your sculpture? What are observers likely to think your sculpture represents?

Decide Were you successful in creating a life-size sculpture that is realistic in scale and proportion? If not, what would you change?

Proportion and Distortion

▲ **Marc Chagall.** (Russian/French).
The Red Horse (Fiesta). 1942.

Gouache on paper. $26\frac{3}{4} \times 19\frac{3}{4}$ inches (67.95×50.17 cm.).
Norton Museum, West Palm Beach, Florida.

Art Criticism · Critical Thinking

Describe **What do you see?**

During this step you will collect information about the subject of the work.

► Describe what you see in Marc Chagall's painting *The Red Horse (Fiesta)*.

Analyze **How is this work organized?**

Think about how the artist used the elements and principles of art.

► Where do you see realistic proportions in this painting? Where do you see unrealistic proportions?

► Do you see examples of distortion?

Interpret **What is the artist trying to say?**

Use the clues you discovered during your analysis to find the message the artist is trying to show.

► What effect does this use of distortion have on the painting?

► How would the painting be different if there were no distortion in it?

► What elements did Chagall use to create mood in this painting?

Decide **What do you think about the work?**

Use all the information you have gathered to decide whether this is a successful work of art.

► Do you see more things hidden in this painting the longer you look at it?

► Do you like how you feel when you view this painting?

Show What You Know

Answer these questions on a separate sheet of paper.

1 _____ is the principle of art that relates to the size relationship of one part to another.
A. Form
B. Proportion
C. Portions

2 When artists create size relationships that do not make sense and look different from usual proportions, they are using _____.
A. realistic scale
B. ratio
C. unrealistic scale

3 _____ is the bending or pulling of an object or figure out of its normal shape to communicate the ideas or feelings of the artist.
A. Distortion
B. Dimension
C. Scale

4 When artists make things bigger than they normally are, they are using _____.
A. proportion
B. miniatures
C. exaggeration

5 A _____ is a comparison of size between two things.
A. realistic scale
B. ratio
C. unrealistic scale

CAREERS IN ART
Jewelry

The art of jewelry making is the creation of ornamental objects, such as bracelets, necklaces, and rings, made with a variety of materials such as metals and gems.

Jewelry designers plan and create pieces of jewelry using materials like gold, silver, and gemstones. They combine their creative ideas with the needs and tastes of their customers to make the jewelry.

Silversmiths and goldsmiths use a metal process known as *annealing*, in which the metals are heated and slowly cooled so they can be bent and manipulated.

Jewelry appraisers decide how much a piece of jewelry is worth and how much it should cost. Because the value of one piece of jewelry can change, a jewelry appraiser must know how the rates are changing in the jewelry market.

▲ **Jeweler**

Proportion and Distortion in Dance

Martha Graham was the most important and enduring dancer and choreographer of the twentieth century. She broke with classical ballet and created her own technique. This dance, "Lamentation," is about a grieving woman. The stretchy cloth worn by the dancer exaggerates her distorted movements, creating powerful expressions of grief.

What to Do Perform a sequence of movements that expresses two contrasting emotions.

Think about the following ideas for expressing action and emotion:

- ▶ reaching upward; sinking downward
- ▶ a change in the tempo of music and actions from fast to slow, and vice versa
- ▶ strong, decisive, energetic motions; peaceful, fluid motions
- ▶ giving up; refusing to give up

Try walking, showing these ideas through posture and gesture.

Experiment with movements that descend and rise, showing these ideas.

Show three different shapes or body postures that capture a moment of grief or joy.

1. Walk, turn, descend, and rise for four counts each.

2. Repeat them, expressing joy. Think about the energy and direction of the movement.

3. Repeat them, expressing grief. Think about the energy and direction of the movement.

4. Do the sequence twice. Decide the order of the two emotions.

▲ Martha Graham. "Lamentation" and "Satyric Festival Song."

Describe Describe the ways in which you distorted movement.

Analyze What choices did you make in sequencing grief and joy?

Interpret Did you experience feelings of joy and grief when you moved?

Decide How successful were you in using distortion to express emotions through dance?

Texture, Rhythm, Movement, and Balance

◀ **Vincent van Gogh.** (Dutch).
Houses at Auvers. 1890.
Oil on canvas. $29\frac{3}{4} \times 24\frac{3}{8}$ inches
(75.56×61.93 cm.). Museum of Fine
Arts, Boston, Massachusetts.

Artists use texture, rhythm, movement, and balance to create interesting works of art.

Vincent van Gogh applied paint so thickly to his
paintings that he created ridges of paint. These raised
areas are real textures that catch light and make his
colors look brighter. He used the principles of rhythm,
movement, and balance to organize the elements in this
landscape painting.

Artists use both real and visual **texture** in their work.

▶ Look at the roofs of the houses in *Houses at Auvers*. How do you think they each might feel if you could touch them?

Artists use **visual rhythm** to help guide the viewer's eyes and to add visual excitement to a work of art.

▶ What lines, shapes, forms, and colors do you see repeated in *Houses at Auvers*?

Movement is used by artists to create rhythm by using positive and negative spaces, similar to musical beats and rests.

▶ What do you see in the painting that is not repeated? Notice how your eyes slow down or even stop when this happens.

Artists organize opposite sides of an artwork to create visual balance.

▶ Notice how the large house on one side is balanced by the bright-colored houses on the other side.

In This Unit you will learn about and practice using texture, rhythm, movement, and balance to create works of art. Here are the concepts you will study:
▶ Texture
▶ Rhythm
▶ Movement through rhythm
▶ Balance

Vincent van Gogh
(1853–1890)

Vincent van Gogh is considered to be one of the most important figures of modern painting. He was one of the first artists to use brightly colored canvases and thick paint to express his feelings. Van Gogh wrote almost daily to his brother Theo, who supplied him with materials. He wrote about his thoughts, feelings, and motivations. Because of these letters, historians have detailed information about the artist and his thoughts.

Lesson 1 Texture

Look at the artwork on these pages. Notice the rough surface of *Memory Jar.* Your eyes tell you what it would feel like if you touched it. George Catlin's painting captures the different textures of the chief's clothing, headdress, and weapon. Can you imagine what these materials would feel like?

◄ **Artist unknown.** (North America). *Memory Jar.* c. 1925.

Mixed media. $8\frac{3}{10} \times 5\frac{1}{2}$ inches (21.07 × 14 cm.). Museum of International Folk Art, Santa Fe, New Mexico.

 Art History and Culture

What can you assume about the subjects and their cultures from viewing the *Memory Jar* and painting?

◀ **George Catlin.** (American).
Mah-To-Tóh-Pa, Four Bears,
Second Chief. 1832.
· ·
Oil on canvas. 29 × 24 inches
(73.66 × 60.96 cm.). Smithsonian
American Art Museum, Washington, D.C.

Study both works of art. Notice how texture is used.

▶ Where do you see a bumpy surface?

▶ Which areas look smooth or shiny?

▶ In which work of art do your eyes tell you how it would feel?

▶ In which work of art could you feel the bumpy surface with your hands?

⊙ Aesthetic Perception

Design Awareness Look around you for surfaces that are made to look like they have a rough texture but are actually smooth.

Using Texture

Texture is the element of art that refers to how things feel, or how they look as if they might feel if they were touched. There are two ways in which we experience texture: by sight and by touch.

Tactile texture is how something actually feels when you touch it.

Visual texture is the way something looks like it might feel if you could touch it. It is the illusion that an artist creates to represent texture.

Tactile Texture

Visual Texture

Practice

Collect items that remind you of the past.

1. Look in different places for items that represent the history of your family.

2. Identify the texture of each item.

3. Choose some of your favorite items and share them with the class.

◀ **Holly Stulb.**
Age 10.

Think about how the artist used texture to create an interesting memory jar.

Creative Expression

How can you save some of your favorite items by incorporating them in a work of art?

1. Collect many small items that reflect your interests.

2. Spread tacky glue on the plastic water bottle.

3. Arrange your collected items on the bottle. Consider texture, contrast, and space.

4. Write a favorite memory on a piece of paper. Place your memory in the memory jar you have created.

5. Place the cap on the bottle. Paint the memory jar using only one color.

 ## Art Criticism

Describe Describe the items that you chose to decorate the memory jar.

Analyze How would you describe the texture of your memory jar?

Interpret What do the items on your memory jar communicate about you?

Decide Are you satisfied with your use of texture on your memory jar?

Rhythm

Look at the artwork on these pages. Notice the puppies that repeat around the bowl and the blue goblets that move your eyes from one side of the painting to the other. The spaces in between these repeated objects give your eyes a rest and help to create a rhythm. In Miró's painting the bold, warm colors are the beats in the rhythm and the cool colors are the rests.

◄ **Paul Gauguin.** (French). *Still Life with Three Puppies.* 1888.

Oil on wood. $36\frac{1}{8} \times 24\frac{5}{8}$ inches (91.75 × 62.53 cm.). Museum of Modern Art, New York, New York.

 Art History and Culture

Surrealism is a twentieth-century style of art in which dreams, fantasy, and imagination are used to create artwork that moves away from realism. Which of these paintings is surreal?

▲ **Joan Miró.** (Spanish).
Hirondelle/Amour.
1933–1934.

Oil on canvas. 78½ × 97½ inches (199.39 × 247.65 cm.). Museum of Modern Art, New York, New York.

Study both works of art to find examples of rhythm.

▶ Which objects or elements do you see repeated in each work of art?

▶ Are there equal amounts of negative space between each repeated object or element?

▶ Imagine that the positive spaces are musical notes and the negative spaces are rests in the music. What kind of musical rhythm do the objects and elements in these paintings convey?

Aesthetic Perception

Seeing Like an Artist Look around you for examples of visual rhythm in natural and man-made designs.

Using Rhythm

Artists create **rhythm** by repeating elements and objects in a work of art.

In music, rhythm is created by the pauses or rests between musical sounds. A beat is followed by a rest.

Visual rhythm is the repetition of shapes, colors, or lines. Rhythm is created by repeated positive spaces that are separated with negative spaces. You can follow visual rhythm with your eyes. The shapes are the beats, and the spaces that separate them are the rests.

Practice

Create rhythm by repeating a shape three times.

1. Find an image of a person in action in a magazine. Cut out the image carefully, removing the excess paper.

2. Trace the cutout image on a piece of warm- or cool-colored construction paper three times. Cut out these shapes.

3. Arrange your shapes so you have equal amounts of space between them. Can you see the beats that are created?

4. Save your shapes to use in the Creative Expression activity.

Think about how this student artist used paper weaving to show rhythm.

Creative Expression

How can you show rhythm using paper weaving? Arrange paper strips on a loom and cut out images to create visual beats.

1. Use paper strips to weave over and under the warp of the prepared paper loom.

2. Glue the ends of the strips down.

3. Space your three cutout images from the Practice activity on your paper weaving to create rhythm.

4. Glue the cutout images in place.

Art Criticism

Describe What color scheme did you use? What activity is your cutout image doing?

Analyze How did you arrange the cutouts to create rhythm?

Interpret Clap out the beat to your completed piece.

Decide Do you feel your work is successful? Explain.

Movement Through Rhythm

Look at the artwork on these pages. Notice the repeated shapes, colors, and elements, and the negative spaces between them in both paintings. Pay attention to how your eyes are moved through the paintings.

▲ **Jennifer Bartlett.** (American).
Swimmer Lost at Night (for Tom Hess).
1978.
....

Two silkscreen pieces on baked-enamel-on-steel units with steel plates and two oil-on-canvas panels.
6 feet 6 inches × 26 feet 5 inches (1.98 × 8.05 m.).
Museum of Modern Art, New York, New York.

 Art History and Culture

Art critics have said that the work of Pablo Picasso influenced Jennifer Bartlett's art. What similarities do you notice in these two works of art? What differences do you see?

Study both works of art for examples of movement through rhythm.

▶ What repeated positive space directs your eyes from one side of Jennifer Bartlett's *Swimmer Lost at Night (for Tom Hess)* to the other?

▶ Where are the negative spaces in this artwork that break up the flow and create a rhythm?

▶ What elements direct your eyes through Pablo Picasso's painting?

▶ Do your eyes move smoothly through this painting, or do they jump around?

◀ **Pablo Picasso.** (Spanish). *"Ma Jolie" (Woman with a Zither or Guitar).* 1911–1912.

Oil on canvas. $39\frac{3}{8} \times 25\frac{3}{4}$ inches (100.03 × 65.41 cm.). Museum of Modern Art, New York, New York.

 Aesthetic Perception

Seeing Like an Artist Notice how some dances have movements that are smooth, slow, and fluid, while others are rigid, quick, and choppy. How would you show these movements in a painting?

Using Movement through Rhythm

Repeated windows on a building make your eyes move across the building. When riding in a car, have you ever noticed fence posts or telephone poles? The repeated posts and poles pull your eyes along as you are driving by. These are examples of movement. **Movement** is the principle of art that leads a viewer's eyes through a work of art.

Artists create **visual movement** in a work of art by repeating elements or objects.

Notice how the repeated lines, shapes, and colors lead your eyes through the scene below.

What objects and elements repeat throughout this picture?

Practice

Make sketches of one object from different points of view.

1. Choose a complex or nonsymmetrical object.
2. Sketch this object from different points of view on one sheet of paper.
3. Make the sketches overlap.
4. Notice the contour changes.

◀ **Seth Rujiraviriyapinyo.**
Age 11.

Think about how the artist created movement by repeating shapes and colors in his cubist-style still life.

Creative Expression

How can you create movement by repeating an element within a work of art? Create a still-life drawing using the cubist style. Repeat shapes and colors to show movement.

1. Select your best sketch and transfer it to your drawing paper.

2. Use a ruler to draw three straight lines crossing the short span of the paper.

3. Use a ruler to draw two straight lines crossing the long span of the paper.

4. Choose cool- or warm-colored pencils, and color in your shapes.

5. Color the background using contrasting colors.

6. Do not let areas of the same color touch one another.

Art Criticism

Describe What objects did you use? What colors did you select for your objects?

Analyze Describe how the repeated shapes and colors create rhythm.

Interpret Explain how the rhythm of the shapes and colors affect the expressive quality of your work.

Decide Do you feel your work is successful? Explain.

Lesson 4 Formal Balance

Look at the artwork on these pages. Imagine a line drawn down the center from the top to the bottom of each painting and compare the opposite sides. Does one side of the painting draw your attention more than the other, or do the sides seem balanced?

◄ **Artist unknown.** (Qing Dynasty). *Portrait of Yinxiang, The First Prince of Yi. (1686–1730).* 1905.

Ink and color on silk. 73½ × 48 inches (186.69 × 121.92 cm.). Arthur M. Sackler Gallery, Smithsonian Institution, Washington, D.C.

 ## Art History and Culture

Diego Rivera is credited with reintroducing fresco painting into modern art in Mexico and the United States. Frescoes are murals painted on fresh plaster.

▲ **Diego Rivera.** (Mexican).
Flower Day. 1925.

Oil on canvas. 58 × 47½ inches
(147.32 × 120.65 cm.). Los Angeles County
Museum of Art, Los Angeles, California.

Study both works of art for examples of balance.

▶ Describe how the objects, colors, and lines are arranged in each work of art. How are they similar? How are they different?

▶ Find the center of each painting. Compare and contrast what you see on the right and left sides.

▶ Are both sides of each painting identical? Where do you see differences?

Aesthetic Perception

Design Awareness Look around your school for examples of things that have been made to look exactly the same on both sides, for example, a basketball or a chalkboard.

Using Formal Balance

Balance is the principle of design that relates to visual weight in a work of art. One type of balance is formal balance.

Formal balance occurs when equal, or very similar, elements are placed on opposite sides of a central line called a central axis.

The **central axis** may be part of the design, or it may be an imaginary line. The central axis, or central line, divides the design in half.

Use an imaginary vertical central axis to divide this photograph. Notice that there is similar weight on both sides, but that they do not look exactly the same.

Symmetry is a special type of formal balance. The two halves of a symmetrically balanced object are the same. They are mirror images of each other.

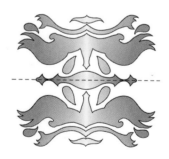

Practice

Draw a formal self-portrait. Use pencil.

1. Fold a piece of drawing paper in half.
2. Look at yourself in a mirror.
3. Draw your self-portrait. Look at the similarities and differences on either side of the central axis.

◄ **Meagan Sheehan.**
Age 10.

Think about how the student artist used formal balance in her self-portrait.

 **Creative Expression**

Use a batik method to create a self-portrait with formal balance.

1. Tape your self-portrait from the Practice activity to the sheet of cardboard.

2. Lay the sheet of fabric over your self-portrait and tape it in place. You should be able to see your drawing through the fabric.

3. Partially open the glue bottle, and practice drawing with the glue on a separate sheet of paper. Carefully trace your self-portrait with glue and allow it to dry.

4. Paint between the glue lines with watercolor paints.

 **Art Criticism**

Describe What colors did you choose to paint your self-portrait? Are they realistic?

Analyze What type of formal balance did you use in your batik self-portrait?

Interpret How does the type of balance you used affect the mood of your self-portrait?

Decide Did you encounter any problems during this project? Explain.

Informal Balance

▲ **Sofonisba Anguissola.** (Italian). *Artist's Sisters Playing Chess and their Governess.* 1555.

Oil on canvas. $28\frac{1}{3} \times 38\frac{1}{5}$ inches. (72 × 97 cm.). Poznań National Museum, Poznań, Poland.

Look at the artwork on these pages. Notice the people and objects that are arranged on each side of the paintings. Are the paintings symmetrical? The artists used different sizes, colors, textures, and positions to balance these paintings.

 Art History and Culture

Sofonisba Anguissola was one of the first women to gain an international reputation as a painter. She worked as a court portraitist from 1559 to 1573 for King Philip II of Spain.

Study both works of art to find examples of informal balance.

► Identify the important figures in each painting.

► How are the figures arranged in these paintings?

► Do some of the figures in these paintings require more attention than others from the viewer?

► Where are the darkest and lightest areas in each painting? How does the placement of these areas affect the mood in each painting?

 James Tissot. (French). *Women of Paris: The Circus Lover.* 1883–1885.

Oil on canvas. 58 × 40 inches (147.32 × 101.6 cm.). Museum of Fine Arts, Boston, Massachusetts.

Aesthetic Perception

Design Awareness Look for examples of informal balance on billboards and other advertisements.

Using Informal Balance

Informal balance is a way of organizing parts of a design so that unlike objects have equal visual weight. Informal balance is also called **asymmetry.** There are several ways that artists create informal or asymmetrical balance.

Size A large shape or form appears to be heavier than a small shape. Several small shapes can balance one large shape. To create informal balance, artists place large shapes close to the center of an artwork and place small shapes farther away.

Color A bright color has more visual weight than a dull color.

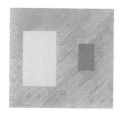

Texture A rough texture has an uneven pattern of highlights and shadows. For this reason, a rough surface attracts the viewer's eyes more easily than a smooth, even surface does.

Position A large positive shape surrounded by a small negative space appears to be heavier than a small positive shape surrounded by a large negative space. Balance can be created by placing a large positive shape close to the center of a scene.

Practice

Demonstrate informal balance.

1. Brainstorm with your group a living scene. Include objects and people that demonstrate informal balance.

2. Model the scene for the class. Be sure to include at least two of the principles explained above.

◀ **Joshua Mellott.**
Age 10.

Think about how the student artist created balance in this artwork.

🎨 Creative Expression

How can you show asymmetrical balance in a still life? Create a still life. Use a printing technique to add color.

1. Arrange the objects you have selected for an asymmetrically balanced still-life.

2. Use your thumb and index finger to form a frame around only one section of the still-life. Lightly draw this section.

3. Use a permanent marker to outline your complete drawing.

4. Paint your tabletop using watercolor paints.

5. Place your drawing right-side down on top of the painted surface. Gently rub the back of your paper and lift it to create a monoprint.

❗❓ Art Criticism

Describe What objects or sections of the still life did you select to draw? What colors did you use?

Analyze Why did you select that particular area of the still life? How did you arrange the objects on your paper?

Interpret What feeling do you get when you look at your asymmetrical still life? Give it a title.

Decide Does your painting show asymmetrical balance? How?

Radial Balance

▲ **Artist unknown.** (Spain). *Deep Dish from Valencia, Spain.* 1430.

Tin-glazed earthenware painted in cobalt blue and lustre. $2\frac{6}{10} \times 19$ inches (6.7 × 48.2 cm.). Hispanic Society of America, New York, New York.

Look at the artwork on these pages. Find the central point of each one and notice how the lines, shapes, colors, and forms are repeated as they move out from the center.

 Art History and Culture

Tin-glaze was used in Mesopotamia in the ninth century. Pottery dipped in a tin-glaze has a surface that colors can be applied to. This type of art reached Spain in the eleventh century under the Moors.

Home Blessing
יִבָרֶכְךָ

G-d has remembered us and will bless us.
He will bless the House of Israel.
May He continue to watch over us and our
children.
May His light shine forth
upon us.

▲ **Noland Anderson.** (American).
Blue Dome-House Blessing. 1955.

Stained and etched glass. 17-inch diameter
(43.18 cm.). Private Collection.

Study both works of art to see examples of
radial balance.

▶ Where is the center of each artwork?

▶ Describe the designs that you see. How are they
arranged?

▶ Can you find where these designs begin and end?

🔍 Aesthetic Perception

Seeing Like an Artist Where do you see examples of radial
balance in nature?

Using Radial Balance

Radial balance occurs when the elements of design (line, shape, color, and form) seem to radiate, or come out from a central point. The elements almost always are spaced evenly around the center of the design and create circular patterns.

Radial balance occurs frequently in nature. Many plants follow radial patterns of growth. Cut an orange in half and you will see the radial pattern of the segments.

People imitate nature in many objects by creating radial designs. You often see radial balance in architecture, such as in round stained-glass windows. The design always radiates out from a central point.

Practice

Create a design using radial balance.

1. With a partner, collect objects in the classroom.
2. Working together, use radial balance to arrange the objects on a desk or table.

◀ **Jansen Sharpe.**
Age 11.

Think about how the artist created a stained glass window design using radial balance.

Creative Expression

How can you use radial balance to create a stained glass window design? Use a computer paint program and a scanner to create radial balance with symmetry.

1. Draw a circle and divide it into eight equal triangular segments. Erase or eliminate all the segments except one.

2. Create a design in the remaining segment using the draw tool and the fill color tool.

3. Copy and paste this segment four times. Select one of the segments created, and using the option button, flip the design horizontally. Copy and paste the design three more times for a total of eight segments.

4. Print the segments. Cut them out and reassemble the segments to form a circular design. Scan the design and print.

Art Criticism

Describe List the steps you followed to make your stained glass window design.

Analyze Explain how this design shows radial balance.

Interpret Explain where and how you could use this design.

Decide Were you successful in creating a design using radial balance?

Texture, Rhythm, Movement, and Balance

▲ **Frida Kahlo.** (Mexican). *Self-Portrait Dedicated to Leon Trotsky.* 1937.

Oil on masonite. 30 × 24 inches (76.2 × 60.96 cm.). National Museum of Women in the Arts, Washington, D.C.

Art Criticism Critical Thinking

Describe **What do you see?**

During this step you will collect information about the subject of the work.

▶ What does the credit line tell us about the painting?

▶ Describe the woman.

Analyze **How is this work organized?**

Think about how the artist has used the elements and principles of art.

▶ Is the texture tactile or visual?

▶ Where do you see repeated lines and shapes that create visual rhythm?

▶ What type of balance is used to organize this work?

Interpret **What is the artist trying to say?**

Use the clues you discovered during your analysis to find the artist's message.

▶ How does the use of formal balance affect the mood of this painting?

▶ Why do you think the woman is posing like this?

Decide **What do you think about the work?**

Use all the information you have gathered to decide whether this is a successful work of art.

▶ Is the work successful because it is realistic, because it is well organized, or because it has a strong message?

Show What You Know

Answer these questions on a separate sheet of paper.

1 _____ is the element of art that refers to how things feel, or how they look as if they might feel if they were touched.
  A. Balance
  B. Texture
  C. Symmetry

2 _____ is the repetition of shapes, colors, or lines.
  A. Musical rhythm
  B. Informal balance
  C. Visual rhythm

3 _____ is the principle of art that leads a viewer's eyes through a work of art.
  A. Movement
  B. Texture
  C. Size

4 _____ occurs when equal, or very similar, elements are placed on opposite sides of a central axis.
  A. Rhythm
  B. Distortion
  C. Formal balance

5 _____ occurs when lines, shapes, colors, and forms seem to radiate, or come out from a central point.
  A. Texture
  B. Radial balance
  C. Blending

VISIT A MUSEUM

The National Museum of Women in the Arts

The National Museum of Women in the Arts holds the largest and most important collection of art by women dating from the sixteenth century. In 1982 Wilhelmina and Wallace Holladay donated their art and library as the foundation of the museum. The museum opened in 1987 in a renovated building in Washington, D.C. In addition to the permanent collection at The National Museum of Women in the Arts, there are special exhibitions and exhibition series that present women artists and their artwork. The museum supports women artists and their changing roles in society. The museum has a library and an extensive research center in which 10,000 artists from all periods and countries are represented.

Texture, Rhythm, and Movement in Dance

This is a photo of a dancer playing a famous outlaw named "Billy the Kid." The ballet about his life and America's Westward movement was choreographed by Eugene Loring. The repeated actions of the dancers create visual rhythm in the dance. Aaron Copland composed the music with musical themes based on old cowboy songs.

What to Do Create a dance or mime using a variety of pioneer work movements.

The ballet *Billy the Kid* uses movement themes taken from pioneer life and work. It shows the Westward movement and the chores that the pioneers did to survive.

1. Select a few ideas to show in mime or movement. Experiment with exaggerating the movement. Create rhythm by repeating actions.

2. Find three ways to vary each work action. Try changing the level, the speed or direction, the movement through space, or the texture of the movements (soft and fluid or choppy and uneven).

3. Select two different actions and build a mime or movement sequence that includes both.

4. Share with a partner. Combine all four ideas and show a perspective of pioneer work life as you perform them together.

▲ Eugene Loring. "Billy the Kid."

Art Criticism

Describe Describe the way you and your partner worked together.

Analyze What things did you do to create visual rhythm in your movements?

Interpret How did it feel to perform the work of pioneers?

Decide Were you successful in creating a pioneer work dance or mime?

Unit 6

Harmony, Variety, Emphasis, and Unity

▲ **Berthe Morisot.** (French).
The Sisters. 1869.

Oil on canvas. $20\frac{1}{2} \times 32$ inches
(52.07 × 81.28 cm.). National Gallery
of Art, Washington, D.C.

Artists use harmony, variety, emphasis, and unity to organize the elements in their work.

Morisot created harmony by posing the two sisters in the same dresses and hairdos. She introduced variety by having them sit in slightly different positions. She emphasized their faces by framing them with the dark brown hair and black necklaces. The balance between harmony and variety unify this work of art.

184   Unit 6

Artists use **harmony** in their artwork to create a feeling of wholeness, or unity, by using separate but related elements.

▶ What elements are repeated in this work of art?

Artists use the principle of **variety** to create difference or contrast in their work.

▶ What objects introduce variety into this work of art?

Emphasis is used by artists to tell the viewer that this element or area is meant to be noticed more than those around it.

▶ How has Berthe Morisot emphasized the fan in this painting?

Artists use the principle of **unity** to tie everything together in a work of art. When a work of art has unity, everything seems to fit together well.

▶ What do you see that ties this work of art together?

In This Unit you will learn about and practice techniques to create harmony, variety, emphasis, and unity to create works of art. Here are the concepts you will study:
▶ Harmony
▶ Variety
▶ Emphasis
▶ Unity

Berthe Morisot
(1841–1895)

Berthe Morisot was born in Bourges, France, and was a member of a group of artists known as the impressionists. She was concerned with creating atmosphere and with reproducing the way light reflected off objects and people. She used a lot of white in her bright scenes of domestic life. During Morisot's painting career, the role of women in society was beginning to change. She incorporated this shift into much of her artwork.

Harmony

▲ **Thomas Hart Benton.** (American).
The Sources of Country Music. 1975.

Acrylic on canvas. 6 × 10 feet (1.82 × 3.05 m.).
Country Music Hall of Fame and Museum,
Nashville, Texas.

Look at the artwork on these pages. Notice the shapes, lines, and colors that are repeated throughout both paintings. Do you see repeated visual texture in each? Think about how this repetition creates unity, or oneness, in the artwork. The parts of the painting seem to fit together because of the harmony that is created.

 Art History and Culture

Thomas Hart Benton was an American regionalist.

▲ **Richard Yarde.** (American).
Savoy: Heel and Toe. 1997.
. . . .
Watercolor. $5 \times 7\frac{1}{4}$ feet (1.52 × 2.2 cm.).
Collection of Denzel and Paulette Washington.

Study both works of art. Notice how harmony is created in each painting.

▶ Look for repeated lines, shapes, colors, and textures in each painting.

▶ Is it easy to tell what the mood is in each painting?

▶ How would you describe the color schemes?

▶ Which scene would you rather be a part of?

Aesthetic Perception

Seeing Like an Artist Look for harmony in outdoor landscapes. Pay attention to repeated line, shape, color, and texture. Think about how designers imitate this natural harmony in their artwork.

Using Harmony

In music, harmony is created when voices blend together to create one unified sound. Artists use harmony, but instead of using combined sounds, they combine the art elements.

Harmony is the principle of art that creates unity by using separate but related elements in an artwork. Artists use harmony in two-dimensional artworks by repeating a shape, color, or texture. Harmony can also work if the space between different shapes, colors, and textures is even.

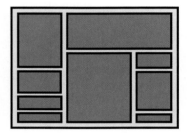

Harmony is created when related shapes of various sizes are repeated. A design using one shape is more harmonious than a design using two or more shapes.

Color creates harmony when a work is limited to only cool or warm colors.

Line creates harmony by limiting lines to either straight or curved lines.

Practice

Find examples of harmony in works of art.

1. With a small group of students, look through the textbook to find examples of harmony of shape, harmony of color, and harmony of line in works of art.

2. Share what you have found with the class.

◄ **Natalie Tucker.**
Age 10.

Think about how the artist created harmony through repeated lines, shapes, and colors.

Creative Expression

How can you show harmony in a mural? Create a painting of objects that are related to a favorite extracurricular activity.

1. Select your best sketch from your Art Journal and draw it large enough to fill the paper.

2. Blend your colors on a mixing tray. Paint your sketched object.

3. Use a fine-line marker to add details to your completed painting.

4. Together with your classmates, create a unified mural.

Art Criticism

Describe Describe the item you chose to paint and how it relates to the theme of the mural.

Analyze What similar art elements do you see in the mural that create harmony within the artwork?

Interpret When a work of art has harmony, what mood does it tend to create?

Decide Is there harmony throughout the mural? Is the theme communicated clearly?

Variety through Difference

▲ **Judith Surowiec.** (American).
Art Teacher. 1996.
. . . .
Acrylic on canvas. 30 × 24 inches
(76.2 × 60.96 cm.). Private collection.

Look at the artwork on these pages. Find the lines, shapes, colors, and textures that are different from one another. Notice the busy students at every table doing different activities in *Art Teacher.* Each person around the table in *Here Look at Mine* is also working on an individual project. Think about how this adds excitement to each painting.

 Art History and Culture

How can you relate to these works of art? Have you ever experienced a similar situation?

▲ **John Robinson.** (American).
Here Look at Mine. 1980.

Acrylic on canvas. 37½ × 26½ inches
(95.25 × 67.31 cm.). The Anacostia
Museum and Center for African
American History and Culture,
Washington, D.C.

Study both works of art. Notice the use of variety in each painting.

▶ How many times can you find an image of the same teacher in *Art Teacher*?

▶ Is she doing the same thing or something different each time she appears in the painting?

▶ Look for different types of lines, shapes, colors, and textures that are placed next to each other in both paintings.

▶ How could you change the colors, shapes, lines, or textures to take the variety out of these paintings and add harmony?

Aesthetic Perception

Design Awareness Look for variety used in architecture. Notice the differences in lines, shapes, colors, media, and textures used for interest in both indoor and outdoor designs.

Using Variety through Difference

Think about walking through a shopping center. The displays, signs, and the way the items are displayed are all varied; they look different from each other. If each store looked the same, or sold the same product, they would have a hard time staying in business. People like to have choices and are attracted to differences.

Artists use variety to add excitement to their work. **Variety** is the principle of art that is concerned with differences or contrasts. It is the opposite of harmony, which deals with similarities or common elements. Variety is created by adding something different to a design to provide a change in the artwork. Lines, shapes, and colors are used to create variety in a work of art.

Practice

Can you discover how photographers use variety in their art?

1. Work with a group to find three examples of photographic images in a magazine.

2. On a sheet of paper, list how the photographers used harmony in each image.

3. Which art element was used most often?

Think about how the artist created variety by changing her image in different places within the artwork.

Creative Expression

How can you create variety in an artwork while using one theme?

1. Look at the sketch you have drawn in your Art Journal.

2. Place yourself three times in this sketch doing normal activities within this chosen school environment.

3. Add objects that clearly communicate who you are in the scene. Keep your clothing the same on all three of your images.

4. Lightly transfer this sketch onto your drawing paper with a pencil. Use colored pencils to complete your drawing.

Art Criticism

Describe Describe the school environment that you chose for your drawing. What objects did you include to communicate who you are in the drawing?

Analyze How did you create variety in this scene?

Interpret What are you doing during the three different times you appear in this scene? Are you communicating different moods in each of the three places?

Decide Were you successful at creating variety in this scene?

Emphasis of an Element

▲ **Arthur Dove.** (American).
Sun. 1943.
....
Wax emulsion on canvas. 24 × 32 inches
(61 × 81.4 cm.). Smithsonian American
Art Museum, Washington, D.C.

Look at the artwork on these pages. Notice how both artists have emphasized, or called your attention to, some parts of the artwork more than others. Sometimes artists use just one element, and other times they combine many to create emphasis in their work.

 Art History and Culture

Mitch Lyons is one of the first artists to extensively explore printing with clay.

▲ **Mitch Lyons.** (American).
Slip Trail. 1997.

Clay monoprint. 22 × 42 inches
(55.88 × 106.68 cm.). Private
Collection.

Study both works of art. Notice the areas of emphasis and how the artists have created them.

► Where do your eyes go first in each artwork?

► What draws your attention to these areas?

► What do you think the artist is trying to communicate through these works of art?

► How would the mood of these works of art be different if they were monochromatic?

Aesthetic Perception

Design Awareness Pay attention to advertisements and how they are designed to get your attention. What has been emphasized to tell you why you should buy their product? Are you convinced?

Using Emphasis of an Element

Have you ever underlined or highlighted an important word? Have you ever noticed in an advertisement how one object is made to appear more noticeable than others around it? This emphasis is meant to direct you to pay attention to an object, or idea. In art, emphasis is used in the same way.

Emphasis is the principle of design that stresses one area in an artwork over another area. Emphasis of an art element is the use of one element, such as line, color, or shape that is meant to be noticed more than the other elements around it. Sometimes the element is made so strong that it seems to take over the entire artwork. The other elements become less important to the viewer.

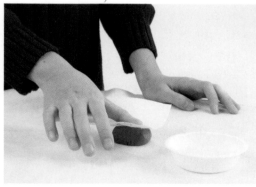

Practice

Create emphasis using lines.

1. Separate a piece of clay into the size of a golf ball.

2. Press the clay flat so that it is the thickness of your thumb.

3. Use a pencil to draw three lines in the clay. Make two lines the same size and width.

4. Use a small amount of water to wet the top of your clay.

5. Place a piece of paper on the top of the clay and rub gently.

6. Peel off the paper. Describe your print. Which line is emphasized?

Kord Miller.
Age 11.

Think about how the artist created emphasis to direct the viewer to a specific area in each print.

Creative Expression

Create a series of three prints emphasizing an art element.

1. Flatten a piece of clay the size of a softball to the thickness of your thumb.

2. Use clay tools to draw repeated lines or shapes in the clay. Press textural materials into the clay and remove.

3. Paint some of your clay design. Spray a little water if the paint begins to dry out.

4. Place paper on the top of the clay plate and rub gently. Carefully peel off.

5. Add more paint. Make two more prints.

6. Label the first print $\frac{1}{3}$, the second $\frac{2}{3}$, and the third $\frac{3}{3}$.

Art Criticism

Describe Describe the lines or shapes you carved into your clay plate. Describe the designs and shapes that were created in the three prints.

Analyze How have you used an art element to create emphasis in your prints?

Interpret Is there a continuous mood throughout all three prints, or does the mood change in each?

Decide Did the prints turn out like you expected them to? How would you change the carvings in the clay plate to achieve a different look in other prints?

Emphasis through Placement

Look at the artwork on these pages. Notice how your eyes are drawn to the center of each artwork.

▲ **Artist unknown.**
(Huichol People/Mexico).
Mother of the Eagles. 1991.
....
Braided yarn embedded in vegetable wax on wood. $15\frac{3}{4} \times 19\frac{1}{2}$ inches (40 × 49.53 cm.). Private collection.

 Art History and Culture

In their artwork, the Huichol people of Mexico often express respect for their native culture with spiritual symbols such as earth, sun, fire, water, wind, corn, deer, and rocks.

Study both works of art. Notice the areas in both pieces that grab your attention. Artists can emphasize an area or an object by placing it alone or toward the center of the artwork.

▶ Where do your eyes go first in each work of art?

▶ How have the artists directed your eyes to these areas?

▶ How might the works of art change if these areas were moved?

▲ **Artist unknown.** (Huichol People/Mexico).
Huichol Bead Mask. 2000.
....
Wood and glass beads. 5 × 3 inches. (12.7 × 7.62 cm.).
Private collection.

Aesthetic Perception

Seeing Like an Artist Look at objects in nature. Record the items that draw your attention to the center. Do you think this area of emphasis affects the survival of this natural object?

Using Emphasis through Placement

You have learned that **emphasis** is the principle of design that stresses one area in an artwork over another area. Two types of visual emphasis can be used: emphasis of an art element and emphasis through placement. Sometimes a specific area in an artwork is emphasized. This area is called the **focal point.** There are several techniques that artists use to create emphasis.

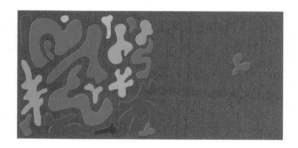

Isolation happens when an object is placed alone and away from the other objects in an artwork. The viewer's eye is drawn to the isolated object.

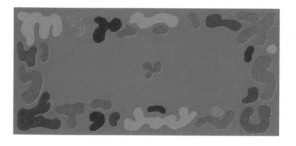

Location occurs when the viewer's eyes are naturally drawn toward the center of an artwork. Anything placed near the center of the picture will be noticed first.

Practice

Look for examples of emphasis in illustrations in literature.

1. Look though picture books with your group for illustrations that have strong focal points or areas of emphasis.

2. Share what you have found with the class.

3. Explain why you chose each illustration and how the artist created emphasis.

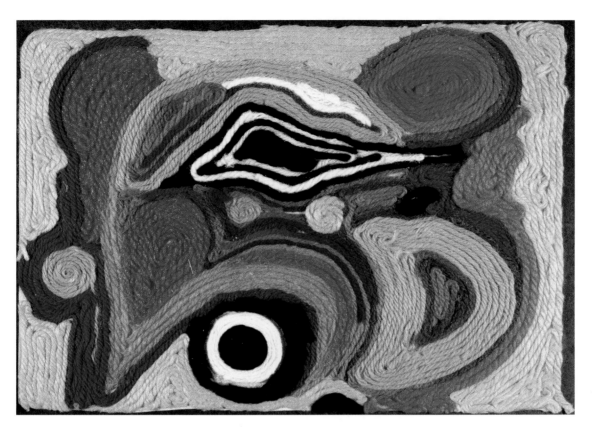

Think about how the artist created emphasis through placement.

🎨 Creative Expression

Create an area of emphasis in an original design through placement using isolation or location.

1. Pick a sketch from your Art Journal and draw it on your cardboard.

2. Place the glue on the outlines of the shapes. Fill in the shapes with strands of different colored yarn. Squeeze a line of glue for each piece of yarn as you work.

3. Use a variety of line directions, yarn, and textures. Do not leave any spaces between the yarn lines.

4. Use a toothpick to press the yarn onto the glued areas.

❗ Art Criticism

Describe Describe the shapes that you used in your design. Are the shapes realistic, or nonobjective?

Analyze How have you created emphasis using placement? Can you find areas of isolation or location?

Interpret Does this work of art communicate a story? What mood is communicated?

Decide Do you have an area of the artwork that turned out better than another? What is it that you like about this area?

Unity through Media

▲ **Irene Preston Miller and the Hudson River Quilters.**
(American). *The Hudson River Quilt.* 1969–1972.

Cotton, wool, and blends with cotton embroidery. $95\frac{1}{4} \times 80$ inches
(241.95 × 203.2 cm.). American Folk Art Museum, New York, New York.

Look at the artwork on these pages. Notice how the artists have used the same materials, or media, throughout their quilts. The scenes created by the artists vary, or are different, as you look at each quilt but the cotton, wool, and embroidery stitching ties the piece together to create unity.

 Art History and Culture

Prior to sewing machines, quilters commonly stitched with hidden stitches. With machines, quilters began to show stitching as a way to boast of owning a sewing machine.

◀ **Elizabeth Garrison.** (American).
Georgia. 1983.

Cotton. 4 × 5¼ feet (1.22 × 1.6 m.)
St. Simons Island Historical Museum of
Georgia, St. Simons Island, Georgia.

Study both works of art. Notice the unity that is created from using the same media, or materials.

▶ What materials were used to make these quilts?

▶ Look at each quilt and find common colors, shapes, lines, and ideas.

▶ How does the repetition of media, materials, and ideas help to bring this artwork together as one piece?

▶ What would change if other materials were added to these quilts? What materials would you add?

Aesthetic Perception

Design Awareness Look at three-dimensional designs, such as bus-stop shelters, and notice how designers have repeated the use of media throughout the design to create unity.

Using Unity through Media

Unity is wholeness, or oneness. Artists create unity by making everything work together. When works of art have unity, all of the elements are arranged to look like they belong together. Artists create unity when they balance the art principles of *harmony*, which stresses similarities, with *variety*, which stresses differences.

Some artists use similar media, or materials, in an artwork to create unity.

Notice how the designer has used bricks in different areas to create unity here.

Quilts are often made up of many different squares, sometimes sewn by many different people, but the entire piece will work together as one artwork because it was created from similar fabric and related materials.

Practice

1. Look through a magazine with a partner. Find objects or sets of objects that have unity because they are made from one kind of media. Look for things like a wood dining room set, matching fabrics, a blanket or quilt made from just one material, a metal filing cabinet, or a set of dishes.

2. Write the characteristics of the object or set of objects that you find.

3. Explain how unity is created through media.

◀ **Kelly Armstrong.**
Age 11.

Think about how the artist created unity through the use of common media.

🎨 Creative Expression

How can you create unity in one artwork made by different people? Make a class quilt using state symbols.

1. Draw your chosen state symbol on a sheet of paper at least four times using different sizes. Color the drawings.

2. Cut each of the symbols out and place them on pieces of construction paper. Trace these shapes with a marker and cut them out.

3. Glue the symbols onto a posterboard square. Place the larger pieces down first. Overlap the shapes.

4. Add details with fine-tip markers.

💬 Art Criticism

Describe Which state did your class choose? What symbol did you choose for this state?

Analyze What media was used to unify this quilt?

Interpret How many symbols can you identify while looking at this state quilt?

Decide What gives this quilt a feeling of harmony? What gives this quilt a feeling of diversity? Do these two elements seem balanced, or is one stronger than the other?

Unity through Theme

▲ **Artist unknown.** (Mexico).
Toy Banks. Twentieth century.
....
Molded, single-fired, and painted earthenware.
$8\frac{1}{4} \times 13$ inches (20.96 × 33.02 cm.). San
Antonio Museum, San Antonio, Texas.

Look at the artwork on these pages and notice
the theme. By using the same theme of animal
banks, the artworks tie together and seem unified.

 Art History and Culture

For thousands of years, clay found in nature has provided Mexican
artists with materials for making sculptures, pottery, and many
other functional, ceremonial, and decorative objects.

◀ **Elizabeth Paulos-Krasle.**
(American). *Puff.* 2003.

14″ inches tall (35.56 cm). Private Collection.

Study both works of art. Notice the theme that brings the works of art together to create unity.

▶ Look at *Toy Banks* and find the common theme that carries throughout the artwork.

▶ What could you add to *Puff* to create unity by continuing a theme?

▶ If you compare *Puff* to *Toy Banks* what theme do you see?

Aesthetic Perception

Seeing Like an Artist Look at different collections and notice the common theme. For example, a collection of sports items might have a team's logo or the mascot on each item.

Using Unity through Theme

Unity is the quality of wholeness or oneness that is achieved by balancing harmony and variety in the elements used. Unity happens when everything seems to tie together. When works of art have unity, all of the elements are arranged to look like they belong together.

Some artists use a similar or common theme in an artwork to create unity. The colors, lines, shapes, and materials might be different, but one theme pulls the artwork together.

Notice how the artist used many different colors, lines, shapes, and materials, but the artwork is unified through the beach theme.

Practice

Practice slip, scoring, and smoothing clay pieces together.

1. Separate clay into two pieces and flatten. Decide which two edges you will reattach.

2. Scratch the two surfaces that will be joined with a tool.

3. Brush the slip, a creamy mixture of clay and water, onto the surface of one of the edges.

4. Gently press the two surfaces together so the slip oozes out of the seam.

5. Use clay tools or your fingers to smooth away the excess slip and smooth the new seam.

◀ **Camila Santos.**
Age 10.

Think about how the artist created unity through a common theme.

Creative Expression

How can you use a common theme to create unity? Design and create a clay animal bank.

1. Create a small pinchpot base in a softball-size ball of clay. Cut a circle a little larger than the size of a quarter in this base.
2. Add clay coils onto the pinchpot for the body of the animal. Score and apply slip between each coil.
3. Make feet and a tail. Add texture and details.
4. Cut a coin slot into the back of the bank.
5. Use a flat tool to smooth the inside of the bank. Stuff newspaper inside the bank to hold the shape until the clay dries.
6. Use a ball of clay the size of a tennis ball to make a small pinch pot for the head.
7. Paint the animal bank.

Art Criticism

Describe What animal did you choose to use for your bank?

Analyze What creates unity in your animal bank?

Interpret What other pieces of art are useful?

Decide Did you change anything from the sketched design as you were working with the clay? Why was this changed? Are you satisfied with the finished product?

Harmony, Variety, Emphasis, and Unity

▲ **Isabel Bishop.** (American). *Subway Scene.* 1957–1958.

Egg tempera and oil on composition board. 40 × 28 inches (101.6 × 71.12 cm.).
Whitney Museum of American Art, New York, New York.

Art Criticism | Critical Thinking

Describe **What do you see?**

During this step you will collect information about the subject of the work.

▶ What does the credit line tell us about the painting?

▶ Where do you see people? Where do you see objects?

Analyze **How is this work organized?**

Think about how the artist has used the elements and principles of art.

▶ What is repeated to create harmony?

▶ Where do you see variety?

▶ What is emphasized?

▶ How did the artist create unity?

Interpret **What is the artist trying to say?**

Use the clues you discovered during your analysis to find the message the artist is trying to show.

▶ Who is this girl and what is she doing? Write a paragraph that describes what she is thinking.

Decide **What do you think about the work?**

Use all the information you gathered to decided whether this is a successful work of art.

▶ Is the work successful because it is realistic, because it is well organized, or because it has a strong message?

Harmony, Variety, Emphasis, and Unity, continued

Show What You Know

Answer these questions on a separate sheet of paper.

1 _____ is the principle of art that creates unity by using separate but related elements such as shape, color, or texture in an artwork.
A. Emphasis
B. Melody
C. Harmony

2 The principle of design that stresses one area in an artwork over another area is _____.
A. Location
B. Variety
C. Unity

3 The principle of design that stresses one area in an artwork over another areas is _____.
A. emphasis
B. media
C. harmony

4 Sometimes a specific area in an artwork is emphasized. This area is called the _____.
A. vanishing point
B. focal point
C. central axis

5 _____ is wholeness or oneness. This is created when the art principles of harmony and variety are balanced.
A. Unity
B. Harmony
C. Placement

CAREERS IN ART
Toy Designers

Think about the many different toys that you have seen and played with. How are these toys different from one another, and what makes them fun?

Toy designers use computer programs to create plans and to brainstorm fresh new ideas for toys. Toy designers consider what materials will be used to make the toys safe and cost effective.

These designers must think about the artistic appeal of the toy. What will make this toy more desirable than other toys? New toys are also expected to be capable of handling many technical functions.

Toy designers are problem solvers who consider cost, technology, age appropriateness, safety concerns, and enjoyment of their products for their customers.

▲ **Toy designer**

Harmony, Variety, Emphasis, and Unity in Dance

▲ Ranganiketan Manipuri Cultural Arts Troupe. "Dhon Dholak Cholam."

The drummers in the photo are from Manipur, India. They work together to play their instruments with unity, variety, emphasis, and harmony. They also dance, doing leaps and turns as they travel around in a circle. The same music has been played for thousands of years, passed on from musician to musician.

What to Do Beat out different rhythm patterns in a "call and response" form.

In India, music is learned by studying with a *guru,* or master teacher. The bond between the teacher and the student is close and respectful. The teacher plays different rhythms and also says them vocally in a "call and response" form. The student repeats the patterns and practices them until the teacher feels he or she is ready to learn more.

1. Sit at a table. Remove everything from the top so it can be used as a drum.

2. Use both hands to beat out short rhythm patterns on the edge of the table. Think of long and short sounds. Emphasize some sounds by making them stronger.

3. Beat out a short rhythmic pattern that you can repeat. Find three patterns you can play.

4. With a partner, take turns being the leader (call) and beating out one pattern at a time. Your partner will repeat each pattern after it has been played (response).

Art Criticism

Describe Describe how a pattern is different from a series of sounds.

Analyze What did you do to create variety and emphasis in your rhythm patterns?

Interpret What feeling did you have when you were the leader? How did you feel as the follower?

Decide Were you able to create rhythmic patterns using a call-and-response form?

Technique Tips

Drawing

Pencil

With a pencil, you can add form to your objects with shading. With the side of your pencil lead, press and shade over areas more than once for darker values. You can also use lines or dots for shading. When lines or dots are drawn close together, darker values are created. When dots or lines are drawn farther apart, lighter values are created.

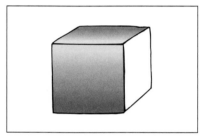

Blending

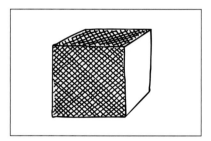

Cross-hatching

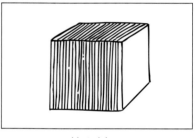

Hatching

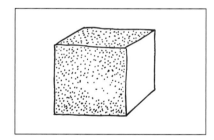

Stippling

Technique Tips

Color Pencil

You can blend colors with color pencils. Color with the lighter color first. Gently color over it with the darker color until you have the effect you want.

With color pencils, you can use the four shading techniques.

Shadows can be created by blending complementary colors.

Technique Tips

Fine-Point Felt-Tip Pen

Fine-point felt-tip pens can be used to make either sketches or finished drawings. They are ideal for contour drawings.

Use the point of a fine-point felt-tip pen to make details.

Fine-point felt-tip pens can be used for hatching, cross-hatching, and stippling.

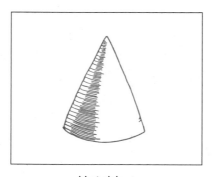

Hatching

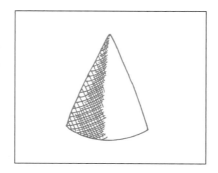

Cross-hatching

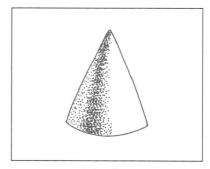

Stippling

Always replace the cap so the fine-point felt-tip pen does not dry out.

Technique Tips

Color Chalk

Color chalks can be used to make colorful, soft designs.

You can use the tip of the color chalk to create lines and shapes and to fill spaces. As with pencil, you can also use them for blending to create shadows.

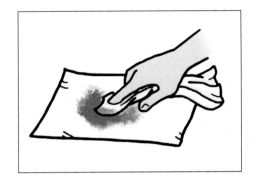

Color chalk is soft and can break easily. Broken pieces are still usable. Colors can be mixed or blended by smearing them together with your finger or a tissue.

Oil Pastels

Oil pastels are colors that are mixed with oil and pressed into sticks. When you press down hard with them, your pictures will look painted.

Oil pastels are soft. You can use oil pastels to color over other media, such as tempera or crayon. Then you can scratch through this covering to create a design.

Charcoal

Charcoal is soft. It can be blended with a piece of rolled paper towel and your finger. Create dark values by coloring over an area several times. Create lighter values by erasing, or by coloring over the charcoal with white chalk.

Technique Tips

Painting

Tempera

1. Fill water containers halfway. Dip your brush in water. Wipe your brush on the inside edge of the container. Then blot it on a paper towel to get rid of extra water. Stir the paints. Add a little water if a color is too thick or dry. Remember to clean your brush before using a new color.

2. Always mix colors on the palette. Put some of each color that you want to mix on the palette. Then add the darker color a little at a time to the lighter color. Change your water when it gets too dark.

3. To create lighter values, add white. To darken a value, add a tiny amount of black. If you have painted something too thickly, add water and blot it with a clean paper towel.

4. Use a thin pointed brush to paint thin lines and details. For thick lines or large areas, press firmly on the tip or use a wide brush.

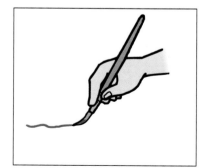

5. Wash your brush when you are finished. Reshape the bristles. Store brushes with bristles up.

Technique Tips

Watercolor

1. Fill water containers halfway. Dip your brush in water. Wipe your brush on the inside edge of the container. Then blot it on a paper towel to get rid of extra water. With your brush, add a drop of water to each watercolor cake and stir. Remember to clean your brush whenever you change colors.

2. Always mix colors on a palette. Put some of each color that you want to mix on the palette. Then add the darker color a little at a time to the lighter color. Change your water when it gets too dark.

3. To create lighter values, add more water. To darken a value, add a tiny amount of black. If you have painted something too quickly, add water to the paint on the paper and blot it with a clean paper towel.

4. Use a thin pointed brush to paint thin lines and details. For thick lines or large areas, press firmly on the tip or use a wide brush.

5. For a softer look, tape your paper to the table with masking tape. Use a wide brush to add water to the paper, working in rows from top to bottom. This is a wash. Let the water soak in a little. Painting on wet paper will create a soft or fuzzy look. For sharper forms or edges, paint on dry paper, using only a little water on your brush.

6. Wash your brushes when you are finished. Reshape the bristles. Store brushes with the bristles up.

Technique Tips

Acrylic Paint

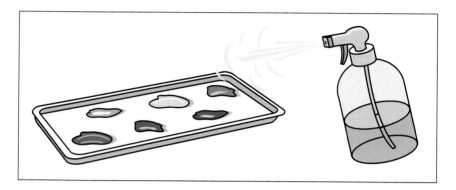

1. Because acrylics dry so fast, squeeze out only a little paint. If you are using a plastic palette, use a spray bottle regularly to spray a fine mist over the paint to keep it moist.

2. Keep a piece of paper towel or cloth next to your water jar, and wipe your brushes on it after you rinse them. When you are not working with your brush, keep it in the water jar.

3. If applied thickly or if mixed with a little white, all acrylic colors can be opaque. If they are diluted, they can be used like watercolors or for airbrushing.

4. Unlike a watercolor wash, when an acrylic wash dries, it is permanent and insoluble. It can be over-painted without disturbing the existing wash.

5. Because acrylics dry rapidly, you need to work fast to blend colors. If you are working on paper, dampening the paper will increase your working time.

6. Masking tape can be put onto and removed from dried acrylic paint without damaging an existing layer. This makes it easy to produce a sharp edge. Be sure the edges of the tape are firmly pressed down. Do not paint too thickly on the edges, or you will not get a clean line when you lift the tape.

7. When you are finished painting, clean your brushes. Be sure to clean inside the bristles so no paint remains.

Technique Tips

Printmaking

Making Stamps

Three methods for making stamps are listed below.
You can cut either a positive or negative shape into
most of these objects. Be sure to talk with your teacher
or another adult about what kinds of tools you can
safely use.

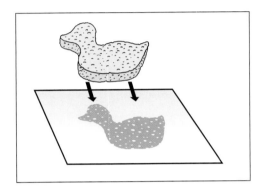

Cut sponges into shapes.

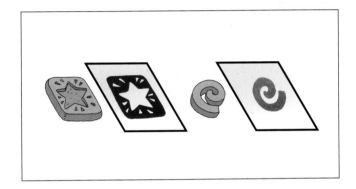

Draw or sculpt a design on a flat piece
of modeling clay. Use a pencil, a clay tool,
the tip of a paper clip, or another object.

Draw or sculpt a design on a
flat piece of plastic foam using
a pencil, the tip of a paper clip,
or another object.

Technique Tips

Printing Stamps

1. Put a small amount of water-based printing ink or some paint onto a hard, flat surface. Roll a softer roller, called a brayer, back and forth in the ink until there is an even coating of paint on both the surface and the brayer.

2. Roll the brayer filled with ink over the printing stamp. The ink should cover the stamp evenly without going into the grooves of your design.

3. You can also use a brush to coat the stamp evenly with paint. Whichever method you use, be careful not to use too much ink or paint.

4. Gently press your stamp onto your paper. Then peel the paper and stamp apart and check your print. If you wish to make several prints of your design, you should ink your stamp again as needed.

5. When you have finished, wash the brayer, the surface, and the stamp.

Technique Tips

Collage

In a collage, objects or pieces of paper, fabric, or other materials are pasted onto a surface to create a work of art. When planning your collage, consider such things as:

- Size of shapes and spaces
- Placement of shapes and spaces
- Color schemes
- Textures

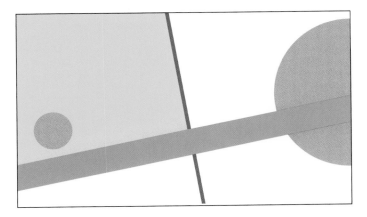

Remember that the empty (negative) spaces are also part of your design. Plan a collage as you would plan a painting or a drawing. After deciding what shapes and objects you want to use, arrange them on the paper. When you have made an arrangement you like, glue, your shapes and objects to the paper.

Technique Tips

Color Tissue Collage

To glue color tissue, mix a solution of one part glue to one part water.

When gluing the tissue, use an old brush to put a small amount of the glue and water solution onto the drawing paper. Next, put the tissue in one place, and brush over the tissue with a small amount of the watered glue. Be careful not to get the color from the tissue on your fingers—the wet tissue is messy and fragile. You can mix colors by overlapping different colored tissues.

Be sure to rinse your brush when you change colors. When you finish, wash the brush with soapy water.

Technique Tips

Sculpting

Papier-Máché

The strip method of papier-máché ("mashed paper") uses paper combined with paste. Often, papier-máché is molded over a form that helps to hold the shape until it is dry.

1. Create a supporting form, if needed. Forms can be made from clay, wadded-up newspaper, cardboard boxes and tubes, balloons, wire, or other materials. Masking tape can be used to hold the form together.

2. Tear paper into strips. Dip the strips into a thick mixture of paste, or rub paste on the strips with your fingers. Use wide strips to cover wide forms, and thin strips or small pieces to cover a small shape.

3. Apply five or six layers of strips. Lay each layer in a different direction so you can keep track of the number of strips and layers. For example, lay the first layer vertically and the second horizontally. Smooth over all rough edges with your fingers. If you are going to leave the form in place permanently, two or three layers of strips should be enough.

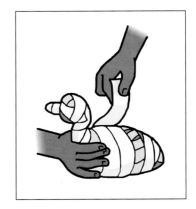

4. When it is dry, you can paint your sculpture.

Technique Tips

Clay

Pinch and pull clay into the desired shape.

Joining Two Pieces of Clay

Score, or scratch, both pieces so they will stick together.

Attach the pieces with some *slip,* which is watery clay.

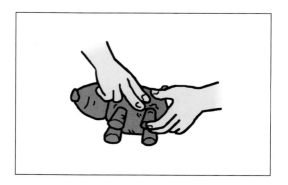

Squeeze the two pieces together.
Smooth the edges.

Technique Tips

Clay Slab Construction

To roll a slab of clay, press a ball of clay into a flat shape on a cloth-covered board. Place one $\frac{1}{4}$-inch slat on each side of the clay. Use a roller to press the slab into an even thickness. With a straightened paper clip, trim the slab into the desired shape.

Wrap unfinished sculptures in plastic to keep them moist until finished.

When you are constructing a form such as a container or house with slabs of clay, it may be necessary to stuff the form with wads of newspaper to support the walls. The newspaper will burn out in the kiln.

Technique Tips

Pinch Pots

To make a clay pinch pot follow the steps below:

1. Make a ball of clay by rolling it between your palms until it is round.

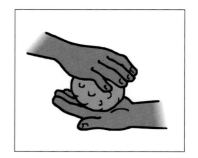

2. Hold the clay ball in your hands and push a thumb into the top of the ball. Stop pushing before you reach the bottom.

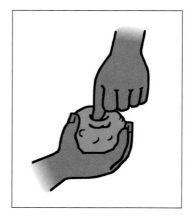

3. Work your way around the clay ball while gently pinching the clay between your thumb and other fingers. Rotate the pot as you pinch.

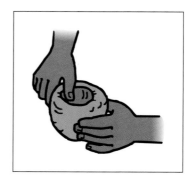

4. Continue pinching and shaping the clay until it develops into the form of a bowl.

Technique Tips

Soft Sculpture

Stuff a stocking or other stretchable material with polyester fill. Sew or glue on buttons, beads, sequins, fabric scraps, and other items to create facial features.

For hair, add yarn, string, or raffia. Try some of the stitches on this page to add details, such as eyebrows, wrinkles, or freckles.

You can use fabric paints for details.

Sew on a real hat, scarf, or head band. Use one of the stitches below.

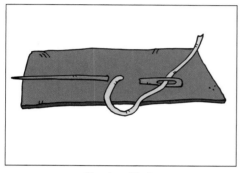

Back stitch

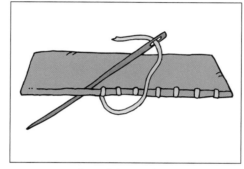

Couching stitch

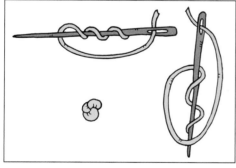

Knotted stitch

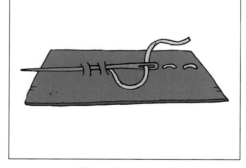

Running stitch

Activity Tips

Expression with Lines

🎨 Creative Expression

1. Think about the five different types of lines. Collect linear mixed-media materials such as yarn, string, and grass.

2. Use different materials to create lines and line variations. Keep in mind the mood that certain lines suggest.

3. Arrange and glue the collage materials onto a piece of cardboard.

Perception Drawing

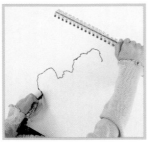

🎨 Creative Expression

1. Look carefully at the posed subjects.

2. Move your pen slowly on your paper while your eyes move around the edges or contours of the subjects.

3. Look at the subjects while you draw, and only glance occasionally at your paper.

4. Do not pick up your pen. Draw in one continuous, unbroken line.

Activity Tips

Unit 1 · Lesson 3   **Geometric and Free-Form Shapes**

Creative Expression

1. Think about objects you might enjoy drawing. Select five or more different sizes and shapes.

2. Arrange the still life. Look for shape, color, and lines.

3. Using a computer, open the paint program and practice using the tools that you will use to draw your still life.

4. Using the paint program, draw the still life. Save and print your finished product.

. . . .

Unit 1 · Lesson 4   **Value with Hatching**

Creative Expression

1. Sketch the models carefully.

2. Use hatching and cross-hatching to indicate value and form.

Activity Tips

Value with Blending

Creative Expression

1. Choose one or more common classroom objects.
2. Notice how much light the surface of these objects reflects. Look for shadows and variations of value.
3. Make line drawings of the objects.
4. Use blending to add form.

Value Contrast

Creative Expression

1. Look around your indoor and outdoor environment. Find an interesting area, with objects or people, that tells a story or expresses a mood.
2. Use a camera. Look through the viewfinder to arrange your composition. Be sure that your photograph will have bright highlights and dark shadows. Take your photograph.
3. Have your photograph developed. Share it with the class.

Activity Tips

Positive and Negative Shapes and Space

🎨 Creative Expression

1. Arrange objects in a still-life pose that have large, interesting negative spaces, such as chairs or desks.

2. Look closely at the still life and find an area of it that you like. Draw what you see. Concentrate on the negative spaces around the objects.

3. Using marker, fill only the negative spaces with color. Leave the positive spaces white.

Space in Two-Dimensional Art

🎨 Creative Expression

1. Think of a place where you like to spend time outside.

2. Draw the scene with chalk, using at least three of the six perspective techniques.

3. Paint your scene.

Activity Tips

Linear Perspective

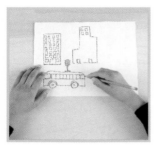

 **Creative Expression**

1. Think of a place you have read about or studied. Make several sketches of objects and two or three buildings you want in your scene.

2. Lightly draw a horizon line. Mark a point where the lines will meet. Draw at least four lines coming out from the vanishing point on the horizon line. Using these guide lines, draw the buildings first, then the objects. Make the objects touch the top and bottom of the guide lines.

3. Paint your drawing.

Shading

 Creative Expression

1. Use simple shapes to sketch your space station. Use the shading techniques to change these shapes into forms.

2. Draw planets. Use blending techniques to move from light to dark. Try complementary colors for shading. Add white highlights.

3. Add an atmosphere by using the side of the oil pastel to make long sweeping marks.

Activity Tips

Form

🎨 Creative Expression

1. Use paper-sculpting techniques, especially scoring and folding, to create forms. Use tab-and-slot techniques with glue to attach the pieces.

2. Cut into the paper without cutting it into two separate pieces.

3. Use markers to draw lines on the sculpture to enhance the edges of the forms.

4. Keep turning the sculpture and adding to the form so that it is interesting from many different points of view.

· ·

Form in Architecture

🎨 Creative Expression

1. Plan the building and its form. Consider what it will be used for.

2. Prepare the materials.

3. Put your building together.

Activity Tips

Monochromatic Colors

🎨 **Creative Expression**

1. From your Art Journal, choose your favorite sketch of a real or imaginary animal that you drew.

2. Draw the animal large, so it fills the entire sheet of construction paper.

3. Color it, using a hue, tints, and shades of that hue, and black and white pastels.

Analogous Colors

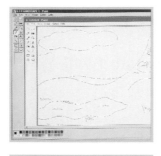

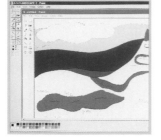

🎨 **Creative Expression**

1. Use the pencil tool in a paint program to create a landscape that includes a foreground, middle ground, and background.

2. Check the colors in the palette for analogous color schemes.

3. Use brush, airbrush, and fill tools to paint the landscape.

Activity Tips

Complementary Colors

Creative Expression

1. Select fruit of like colors.

2. Refer to the sketches in your Art Journal and draw the fruit using different sizes and shapes on squares of paper.

3. Paint the fruit with shades and tints of one chosen hue.

4. Cut out the fruit shapes.

5. Arrange and glue the fruit on a complementary-colored background.

Warm and Cool Colors

Creative Expression

1. Think about warm and cool colors you like.

2. Cut free-form and geometric shapes out of colored drawing paper and tissue paper.

3. Arrange your shapes on white paper. Combine the warm and cool colors. Allow the tissue-paper shapes to overlap some of the drawing-paper shapes.

4. Use a glue water wash to attach your shapes onto the white background.

Activity Tips

Pattern

🎨 Creative Expression

1. Choose your favorite motif sketch and draw it on a foam printing plate.
2. Cut out the motif and add details by etching lines with a ballpoint pen.
3. Place some ink on the inking plate. Spread out the ink using a brayer.
4. Use the brayer to roll ink onto the foam printing plate. Repeat this until you have filled the paper with a random arrangement of prints.
5. After the print is dry, use oil pastels to add details.

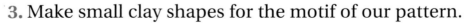

Decorative Pattern

🎨 Creative Expression

1. Make a small clay ball, and press it flat to make the base of your bowl.
2. Using a flat hand, roll pieces of clay in one direction into coils. Stack the coils on top of one another to make the walls of the bowl. Smooth out the inside coils to join them all together.
3. Make small clay shapes for the motif of our pattern.
4. Attach the motifs to the outside coils using slip and scoring techniques.
5. Scratch lines in the clay to enhance the pattern.

Activity Tips

Proportion

🎨 Creative Expression

1. Think about proportion as it relates to people. Use the sighting technique to determine the proportion of your model.

2. Use chalk and a soft eraser to lightly sketch your model.

3. Add color to your drawing by covering over all the chalk lines with oil pastels.

. . . .

Scale

🎨 Creative Expression

1. Think about an indoor or outdoor background to use in your collage and the object that you will add. Cut out pictures of objects, some that are in proper scale and one or two that are too large or too small for the other objects.

2. Arrange your collected images so that they overlap and touch the edges of your paper. Keep the arrangement organized so that it is almost realistic.

3. Glue down the background. Next glue the remaining objects. Make sure that at least one object shows unrealistic scale.

Activity Tips

Face Proportions

Creative Expression

1. Think about the shape and size of your partner's head.

2. Measure the size of your partner's head. Mark off the dimensions on paper. Next, lightly draw guide lines for the eyes. Keep proportion in mind.

3. Draw the hair, eyebrows, clothing, the neck, and shoulders.

4. Paint the portrait using watercolor paints.

Distortion of Body Proportions

Creative Expression

1. Think about comic-strip characters you are familiar with. Then make several sketches of your own original comic-strip superhero.

2. Choose one sketch. Distort one or more body features to show the superpower of your character. Give your character a name.

Activity Tips

Distortion of Face Proportions

Creative Expression

1. Tear one-inch strips of newspaper. Dip the strips into paste and squeeze off the excess liquid. Lay the strips over the outside of a plastic milk container. Overlap two layers of newspaper strips to make the base of your mask.

2. Allow the base to dry, then add the features. Distort the features. Apply two more layers of papier-mâché, and let the mask base dry overnight.

3. When it is dry, pop your mask off the container and trim the edges. Paint the mask and apply other objects.

Scale and Proportion

Creative Expression

1. Think about available items you have to make a life-size soft sculpture. Work in small groups. Plan and make sketches of your figure and of the environment.

2. Divide responsibilities. For example, some students can create a soft-sculpture head while others stuff clothes with newspaper. Others can construct the environment. Make sure your figure is in scale with the environment.

3. Make a sign that gives the title and the students' names who created the sculpture.

Activity Tips

Texture

Creative Expression

1. Collect many small items that reflect your interests.
2. Spread tacky glue on the plastic water bottle.
3. Arrange your collected items on the bottle. Consider texture, contrast, and space.
4. Write a favorite memory on a piece of paper. Place your memory in the memory jar you have created.
5. Place the cap on the bottle. Paint the memory jar using only one color.

Rhythm

Creative Expression

1. Use paper strips to weave over and under the warp of the prepared paper loom.
2. Glue the ends of the strips down.
3. Space your three cutout images from the Practice activity on your paper weaving to create rhythm.
4. Glue the cutout images in place.

Activity Tips

Movement through Rhythm

 **Creative Expression**

1. Select your best sketch and transfer it to your drawing paper.
2. Use a ruler to draw three straight lines crossing the short span of the paper.
3. Use a ruler to draw two straight lines crossing the long span of the paper.
4. Choose cool- or warm-colored pencils, and color in your object.
5. Color the background using contrasting colors.
6. Do not let areas of the same color touch one another.

Formal Balance

 **Creative Expression**

1. Tape your self-portrait from the Practice activity to the sheet of cardboard.
2. Lay the sheet of fabric over your self-portrait and tape it in place. You should be able to see your drawing through the fabric.
3. Partially open the glue bottle, and practice drawing with the glue on a separate sheet of paper. Carefully trace your self-portrait with glue and allow it to dry.
4. Paint between the glue lines with watercolor paints.

Activity Tips

Informal Balance

🎨 Creative Expression

1. Collect and arrange objects. Use your thumb and index finger to form a frame around the still life to help you look at only one section of it. Lightly draw your selected section of the still life.

2. Use a permanent marker to outline your complete drawing.

3. Decide on a color scheme. Paint your tabletop using watercolor paints.

4. Place your drawing right-side down on top of the painted surface. Gently rub the back of your paper and lift it to create a monoprint.

Radial Balance

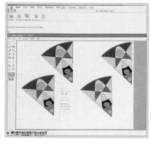

🎨 Creative Expression

1. Draw a circle and divide it into eight equal triangular segments. Erase or eliminate all the segments except one.

2. Create a design in the remaining segment using the draw tool and the fill color tool.

3. Copy and paste this segment four times. Select one of the segments created and using the option button, flip the design horizontally. Copy and paste the design three more times for a total of eight segments.

3. Print the segments. Cut them out and reassemble the segments to form a circular design. Scan the design and print.

Activity Tips

Harmony

 **Creative Expression**

1. Select your best sketch from your Art Journal and draw it large enough to fill the paper.

2. Blend your colors on a mixing tray. Paint your sketched object.

3. Use a fine-line marker to add details to your completed painting.

4. Together with your classmates, create a unified mural.

Unit 6 · Lesson 2 **Variety through Difference**

Creative Expression

1. Look at the sketch you have drawn in your Art Journal.

2. Place yourself three times in this sketch showing you doing normal activities within this chosen school environment.

3. Add objects that clearly communicate who you are in the scene. Keep your clothing the same in all three of your images.

4. Lightly transfer this sketch onto your drawing paper with a pencil. Use colored pencils to complete your drawing.

Activity Tips

Emphasis of an Element

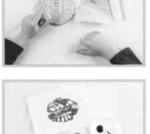

 **Creative Expression**

1. Use a piece of clay the size of a softball. Flatten it with the palms of your hands to equal the thickness of your thumb.

2. Use clay tools to draw repeated lines or shapes in the clay. Add texture by pressing textural materials into the clay and removing.

3. Paint some of your clay design. Spray a little water if the paint begins to dry out.

4. Place a piece of paper on the top of your clay plate and rub gently. Carefully peel off the paper.

5. Add more paint, making two more prints.

Emphasis through Placement

Creative Expression

1. Pick a sketch from your Art Journal and draw it on your cardboard.

2. Place the glue onto the outlines of the shapes. Fill in the shapes with strands of different-colored yarn. Squeeze a line of glue for each piece of yarn as you work.

3. Use a variety of line directions, yarn, and textures. Do not leave any spaces between the yarn lines, and be sure that no cardboard is showing.

4. Use a toothpick to press the yarn onto the glued areas.

Activity Tips

Unity through Media

🎨 Creative Expression

1. Draw your chosen state symbol on a sheet of paper at least four times in four different sizes. Color the drawings.

2. Cut out each symbol and place them on pieces of construction paper. The color of the construction paper should match the color used in your drawings. Trace these shapes with a black felt marker on the construction paper and cut them out.

3. Glue the symbols onto a posterboard square. Use fine-tipped markers to add detail to your quilt square.

Unity through Theme

🎨 Creative Expression

1. Use your thumb to create a small pinchpot base in a ball of clay the size of a softball. Cut a circle a little larger than the size of a quarter in this base.

2. Make clay coils to build onto the pinchpot for the body of the animal. Narrow the figure as you approach the neck. Cut a coin slot a little larger than the size of a quarter into the back of the bank.

3. Add a head, feet, and a tail. Add texture and details.

4. Paint the animal bank after it has been fired.

Visual Index

Artist Unknown
Mask
12th–9th century
B.C. (page 143)

Artist Unknown
Half of a Tunic
A.D. 600–900.
(page 112)

Artist Unknown
Featherwork Neckpiece
c. 1350–1476.
(page 104)

Artist Unknown
*Deep Dish from
Valencia, Spain*
1430. (page 176)

Domenico Ghirlandaio
*Francesco Sasetti and His
Son Teodoro*
c. 1480. (page 130)

Sofonisba Anguissola
*Artist's Sisters Playing
Chess and their Governess*
1555. (page 172)

Lavinia Fontana
*Portrait of a
Noblewoman*
c. 1600. (page 94)

Nanha
*Emperor Shah Jahan and
His Son, Suja*
1625–1630. (page 131)

Jan Vermeer
The Concert
1665–1667. (page 64)

Charles James
Sun Transformation Mask
early 19th century.
(page 142)

Artist Unknown
Kwele Face Mask
c. 19th–20th century.
(page 143)

George Catlin
Mah-To-Tóh-Pa, Four Bears,
Second Chief
1832. (page 157)

James McNeill Whistler
Weary
1863. (page 49)

Berthe Morisot
The Sisters
1869. (page 184)

Winslow Homer
Nooning
c. 1872. (page 70)

William Adolphe Bouguereau
The Nut Gatherers
1882. (page 71)

James Tissot
Women of Paris: The
Circus Lover
1883–1885. (page 173)

Edgar Degas
Ballerinas
1885. (page 40)

Paul Cézanne
Pierrot and Harlequin
1888. (page 120)

Paul Gauguin
Still Life with Three Puppies
1888. (page 160)

Artist Unknown
Navajo Blanket Eye Dazzler
1890. (page 101)

Vincent van Gogh
House at Auvers
1890. (page 154)

Louis Sullivan
Elevator Grill
1893–1894. (page 117)

Paul Cézanne
Still Life with Basket of Apples
1895. (page 45)

Henri de Toulouse-Lautrec
Madame Thadée Natanson at the Theater
1895. (page 41)

Artist Unknown
Bowl
Late 19th–early 20th century. (page 116)

Artist Unknown
Toy Banks
early 20th century. (page 206)

Artist Unknown
Portrait of Yinxiang,
The First Prince of Yi
1905. (page 168)

Childe Hassam
Lower Manhattan
(View Down Broad
Street)
1907. (page 74)

Pablo Picasso
"Ma Joli" (Woman with
a Zither or Guitar)
1911–1912. (page 165)

Paul Strand
From the Viaduct,
125th St.
1916. (page 56)

Robert Henri
Tilly
1917. (page 135)

Amedeo Modigliani
Portrait of a Polish
Woman
1918. (page 139)

Diego Rivera
Study of a Sleeping
Woman
1921. (page 53)

Raoul Dufy
Fenetre Ouverte Devant
la Mer (Window Open to
the Sea)
1923. (page 108)

Artist Unknown
Memory Jar
c. 1925. (page 156)

Diego Rivera
Flower Day
1925. (page 169)

Raoul Dufy
Open Window, Nice
1928. (page 60)

John Steuart Curry
Tornado Over Kansas
1929. (page 126)

Joan Miró
Hirondelle/Amour
1933–1934. (page 161)

Charles Sheeler
Feline Felicity
1934. (page 52)

Georges Braque
*Still Life on Red
Tablecloth*
1936. (page 44)

Frida Kahlo
*Self-Portrait Dedicated
to Leon Trotsky*
1937. (page 180)

Elon Webster
False Face Mask
1937. (page 142)

Georgia O'Keeffe
*Red and Pink Rocks
and Teeth*
1938. (page 100)

Marc Chagall
The Red Horse (Fiesta)
1942. (page 150)

Arthur Dove
Sun
1943. (page 194)

George Tooker
Bird Watchers
1948. (page 127)

Le Corbusier
Chapelle de Notre-Dame du Haut
1950–1955. (page 86)

Artist Unknown
Ceremonial Panel
1950–1975. (page 113)

Artist Unknown
Huipil Weaving
c. 1950. (page 36)

Jackson Pollock
Convergence
1952. (page 37)

Isabel Bishop
Subway Scene
1957–1958. (page 210)

Ansel Adams
Aspens, Northern New Mexico
1958 (Print 1976). (page 57)

Manabu Mabe
Melancholy Metropolis
1961. (page 109)

Marisol Escobar
The Family
1962. (page 90)

Jasper Johns
Map
1962. (page 97)

Fernando Botero
Ruben's Wife
1963. (page 138)

Robert McCall
Space Station #1
c. 1968. (page 79)

**Irene Preston Miller
and the Hudson River Quilters**
The Hudson River Quilt
1969–1972. (page 202)

Elizabeth Catlett
Sharecropper
1970. (page 48)

Tony Smith
Gracehoper
1971. (page 83)

Ben Jones
King Family
1971. (page 96)

Jasper Johns
Cups 4 Picasso
1972. (page 66)

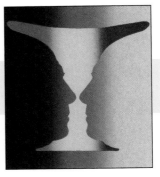

Jasper Johns
Cups 4 Picasso
1972. (page 67)

Jørn Oberg Utzon
Opera House
1973. (page 87)

Thomas Hart Benton
The Sources of Country Music
1975. (page 186)

George Segal
Walk Don't Walk
1976. (page 146)

Jennifer Bartlett
Swimmer Lost at Night (for Tom Hess)
1978. (page 164)

John Robinson
Here Look at Mine
1980. (page 191)

Duane Hanson
Football Player
1981. (page 147)

Viola Frey
Grandmother Series:
July Cone Hat
1982. (page 124)

Elizabeth Garrison
Georgia
1983. (page 203)

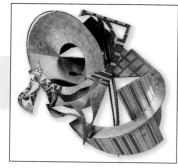

Frank Stella
St. Michaels Counterguard
1984. (page 82)

Roger Brown
Homesick Proof Space Station
1987. (page 78)

Artist Unknown
Mother of the Eagles
1991. (page 198)

Elizabeth Catlett
Singing Their Songs
1992. (page 134)

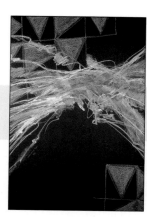

Willis "Bing" Davis
Ancestral Spirit Dance
#187
1994. (page 105)

Noland Anderson
Blue Dome-House Blessings
1995. (page 177)

Jaune Quick-to-See Smith
Spam
1995. (page 34)

Judith Surowiec
Art Teacher
1996. (page 190)

Mitch Lyons
Slip Trail
1997. (page 195)

Richard Yarde
Savoy: Heel and Toe
1997. (page 187)

Frederick Brosen
Watts Street
1998. (page 75)

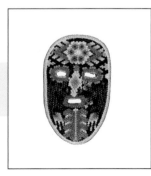

Artist Unknown
Huichol Bead Mask
2000. (page 199)

Elizabeth Paulos Krasle
Puff
2003. (page 207)

Glossary

A

alternating pattern
(ôl' tər nāt ing pat' ərn), *noun* Can repeat a motif, but change position; alter spacing between motifs or add a second motif

analogous colors
(ə nal' ə gəs kul' ərs), *noun* Colors that sit side by side on the color wheel and have a common hue. Violet, blue-violet, blue, blue-green are examples of analogous colors.

approximate symmetry
(ə 'präk sə mət sim' i trē), *noun* A type of formal balance that is almost symmetrical but small differences in the artwork make it more interesting

architects (är' kə tekts), *noun* Artists who design buildings, cities, and bridges using three-dimensional forms

architecture (är' kə tek' chər), *noun* The art of designing and planning buildings, cities, and buildings

assemblage (ä säm bläzh'), *noun* A sculpture technique in which a variety of objects is assembled to create one complete piece

asymmetry (ā sim' i trē), *noun* Another name for informal balance. Something asymmetrical looks balanced even if it is not the same on both sides.

B

background (bak' ground'), *noun* The area of the picture plane farthest from the viewer

balance (bal' ə ns), *noun* The principle of design that deals with visual weight in an artwork

blending (blen ding), *noun* A shading technique that creates a gradual change from light to dark or dark to light

body proportions
(bod' ē prə pôr shənz), *noun* The size relationship of one part of the body to another

C

central axis (sen' trəl ak' sis), *noun* A real or imaginary dividing line which can run in two directions, vertically and horizontally

collage (kō läzh), *noun* A two-dimensional work of art made up of pieces of paper and/or fabric to create the image.

color (kul' ər), *noun* 1. The art element that is derived from reflected light; 2. In balance: a brighter color has more visual weight than a dull color; 3. In perspective: bright-colored objects seem closer, while dull or pale objects appear farther away.

color intensity (kul' ər in tem' si tē), *noun* The brightness or dullness of a color

color scheme (kul' ər skēm'), *noun* A plan for organizing the colors used in an artwork

color spectrum (kul' ər spek' trum), *noun* The effect that occurs when light passes through a prism and separates into a band of colors in the order of red, orange, yellow, green, blue, and violet

color wheel (kul' ər 'wēl), *noun* Shows the color spectrum bent into a circle

complementary colors (kom' plə men tə rē kul' ərz), *noun* Colors that are opposite each other on the color wheel

complex geometric shapes (kom' pleks jē' ə met' rik shāps), *noun* Combined basic geometric shapes: a pentagon or hexagon

contour (kon' tür), *noun* The edges and surface ridges of an object or figure

contour lines (kon' tür līnz), *noun* Continuous, unbroken lines that show the edges and surface ridges of an object or figure

contrast (kon' trast), *noun* 1. A technique for creating a focal point or area of interest in a work of art using differences in elements; 2. In emphasis: contrast occurs when one element stands out from the rest of the work.

converging (kən' vərg ing), *adj.* (verb) Coming together at one point or place

converging lines (kən vərg ing līnz), *noun* One of the six perspective techniques. Parallel lines seem to converge or move toward the same point as they move away from you.

cool colors (kül kul' erz), *noun* Green, violet, and blue. They suggest coolness and move away from the viewer.

cross-hatching (krôs hach' ing), *noun* A shading technique created when sets of parallel lines cross or intersect

curling (kərl), *verb* Hold one end of a long strip of paper. Grip the middle of the paper strip next to the side of a pencil. With a quick motion, pull the strip firmly across the pencil.

curved (kûrvd), *adj.* Lines that bend and change gradually or turn inward to form spirals

D

detail (dē tāl), *noun*   One of the six perspective techniques. Objects with fuzzy, blurred edges appear farther away than those with clear sharp edges.

decorative (de kē rā tiv), *adj.* Serving to make more beautiful; to adorn with ornaments

depth (depth), *noun.*   The appearance of distance in a two-dimensional artwork

diagonal (dī ag' ə nəl), *noun* (adj.) Lines that move on a slant

distortion (di stôr shən), *noun* A deviation from normal or expected proportions

E

emphasis (em' fə sis), *noun*   The principle of design that stresses one area in an art work over another area

exaggeration (eg zaj' ə rā' shən), *noun*   To increase or enlarge beyond what is expected or normal

F

face proportions (fās prə pôr shənz), *noun*   The relationship of one feature of a face to another feature

focal point (fo' kəl point'), *noun* The point which the receding lines meet. It is the first part of a composition to attract the viewer's attention

foreground (fôr' ground'), *noun* The area of the picture plane that is closest to the viewer

form (form), *noun*   A three-dimensional object that is measured by height, width, and depth

formal balance (fôr' mel bal' əns), *noun*   Occurs when equal or similar elements are placed on opposite sides of a central axis

free-form forms (frē' fôrm' fôrmz), *noun*   Three-dimensional forms with irregular edges often found in nature

free-form shapes (frē' fôrm' shāps), *noun*   Two-dimensional images made of straight or curved lines or a combination of both

freestanding sculpture (frē stan' ding skulp' chər), *noun*   A three-dimensional work of art that can be viewed on all sides because it is surrounded by space

fringing (frinj ing), *verb*   Make parallel straight cuts along the edge of a piece of paper to create a ruffled look.

G

geometric forms (je' ə met' rik fôrmz), *noun*   Mathematically precise forms based on geometric shapes

geometric shapes (je' ə met' rik shāps), *noun* Mathematically precise shapes: circle, square, and triangle

gesture lines
(jes' chər līnz), *noun* Lines drawn quickly to capture the movement of a person, animal or object

gesture sketch
(jes' chər skech), *noun* Quick drawings used to capture the position or movement of the body

guide lines (gīd līnz), *noun*
Lines used by artists to create both full-face and profile portraits more accurately

H

harmony (här' mə nē), *noun* The principle of art which creates unity by stressing similarities of separate but related parts

hatching (hach' ing), *noun*
A shading technique that looks like a series of parallel lines

highlights (hī līts), *noun* Small areas of white or light value to show the brightest spots

horizon line (hər' ī zən līn), *noun*
The point at which the earth and sky meet. The horizon line is always at the viewer's eye level.

horizontal (hôr' ə zon təl), *noun*
Lines that move from side to side

hue (hū), *noun* Another name for color

I

informal balance (in fôr'məl bal' əns), *noun* A way of organizing parts of a design so that unlike objects have equal visual weight

intermediate hues
(in' tər m' de it hūz), *noun* Yellow-green, red-orange, blue-green, made by combining a primary with either of the secondary hues that are adjacent on the color wheel

isolation (ī' sə lā' shən), *noun* An object is emphasized by its placement apart from other objects.

L

line (līn), *noun* The path of a moving point through space

linear perspective
(lin ē' ər pər spek' tiv), *noun*
A system used to create the illusion of depth on a flat surface

location (lō cā' shən), *noun*
Artists can emphasize an object by placing it closer to the center of the piece.

M

mandala (mən də lə), *noun* A radial design divided into sections or wedges, each of which contains a different image

middle ground (mid' əl ground'), *noun* The area of the picture plane that is usually towards the center

mixed-media (mikst mē dē' ə), *noun* An art object that has been created from an assortment of media or materials

motif (mō tēf), *noun* A unit that is made up of objects or art elements which is repeated

monochromatic
(mon' ə kro mat' ik), *adj.*   A color scheme which is made up of one hue and the tints and shade of that hue

movement (müv' mənt), *noun*
The principle of art that leads a viewer's eyes throughout a work of art

N

negative space (neg' ə tiv spas'), *noun*   The empty space that surrounds objects, shapes, and forms

nonobjective (non' əb jek' tiv), *adj.*
Art that has no recognizable subject matter

O

one-point linear perspective
(wun' point lin ē' ər pər spek' tiv), *noun*   A system used to create the illusion of depth on a flat surface where all receding lines meet at one point

opaque (ō pāk'), *adj.*   Does not let light through

overlapping (o' vər lap ing), *noun*
1. One object covers a portion of another object. 2. In perspective: one of the perspective techniques, the object covering another will appear closer to the viewer, creating a feeling of depth.

P

paper sculpting techniques
(pā pər skəlpt ing tek nēks), *noun*
Six different techniques used to create paper sculptures: scoring a straight line, scoring a curve, pleating, curling, fringing, tab and slot.

parallel lines (per ə lel līnz), *noun*
Lines that move in the same direction and always stay the same distance apart

pattern (pat' ərn), *noun*
A repeated surface decoration

perception drawing
(pər səp shən drô' ing), *verb*
Looking at something carefully and thinking deeply about what you see as you draw

perspective
(pər spek' tiv), *noun*   The method used to create the illusion of depth in two-dimensional art: overlapping, size, placement, detail, color, converging lines

picture plane (pik' chər plān'), *noun*   The surface of a drawing or painting.

placement (pləs ment), *noun*   One of the six perspective techniques. Objects placed lower in the picture appear to be closer than those placed near eye level. There are three areas on a picture plane: foreground, middle ground, and background.

pleating (plēt' ing), *verb*   Fold piece of paper from edge ro edge. Then fold the same amount of paper in the other direction. Continue folding back and for the in this manner.

portrait (por trət), *noun*   A two- or three-dimensional artwork created in the image of a person or animal

position (pə zish' ən), *noun*   In balance: a larger, positive shape and a small, negative space can be balanced by a small, positive shape and a large, negative space.

positive space (poz' i tiv spas'), *noun*   Refers to any object, shape, or form in two- and three-dimensional art

primary hues (pri' mer ē hūz), *noun*   Red, yellow, and blue, used to mix the other hues on the color wheel

profile (prō fīl), *noun*   A side view of a person or animal

profile proportions (prō fīl prə pôr' shənz), *noun*   A side view of the head that is divided by three horizontal lines

proportion (prə pôr' shən), *noun*   The principle of art that is concerned with the size relationship of one part to another

R

radial balance (rā' dē əl bal' əns), *noun*   A type of balance that occurs when the art elements come out, or radiate, from a central point

random pattern (ran' dəm pat' ərn), *noun*   Occurs when the motif is repeated in no apparent order

ratio (rā shē ō), *noun*   A comparison of size between two things

realistic scale (rē ə lis' tik skāl), *noun*   When an artist creates a work of art where everything fits together and makes sense in size relation

regular pattern (reg' yə lər pat' ərn), *noun*   Occurs when identical motifs are repeated with an equal amount of space between them

relief sculpture (ri ləf' skulp' chər), *noun*   A sculpture in which objects stick out from a flat surface

rhythm (rith' əm), *noun*   The principle of design that organizes the elements in a work of art by repeating elements and/or objects

S

scale (skāl), *noun*   Size as measured against a standard reference

score (skor), *verb*   The repeated scratching of the clay surface at the area that another scored piece will be attached

scoring a curve (skor' ing ā kûrv), *verb*   Gradually cut bending curves in the paper with the point of the scissors

scoring a straight line (skor' ing ā strāt līn), *verb*   Hold a ruler in the center of a piece of paper. Run the point of the scissors along the edge of the ruler to cut the paper in a straight line.

secondary hues (sek' ən der' ē həz), *noun*   Orange, green and violet; the result of mixing two primary hues

self-portrait (self por trət), *noun* A two or three-dimensional artwork that an artist makes of him or herself

shade (shād), *noun* Any hue blended with black

shading (shād ing), *verb* Use of dark values to create the illusion of form and texture

shadows (sha dōz), *noun* Shaded areas in a painting or drawing

shape (shāp) *noun* A two-dimensional area that is measured by height and width

shape reversal (shāp rē ver səl) *noun* Occurs when an object, shape or form is positive space in one image and then in another image becomes negative space

size (sīz), *noun* 1. In perspective: objects that are closer look larger than objects that are farther away; 2. In balance: a large shape or form will appear to be heavier than a small shape, and several small shapes can balance one large shape.

slip (slip), *noun* A mixture of clay and water that is creamy to the touch and is used to attach two scored pieces of clay together

space (spās), *noun* The art element that refers to the areas above, below, between, within, and around an object

still life (stil' līf'), *noun* The arrangement of common inanimate objects from which artists draw or paint

stippling (stip' ling), *noun* A shading technique using dots to show value

symmetry (sim' i trē), *noun* A type of formal balance in which two halves of a balanced artwork are identical, mirror images of each other

T

tactile texture (tak' təl teks' chər), *noun* Actual texture, texture that can really be felt

texture (teks' chər), *noun* 1. The art element that refers to the way something feels; 2. In balance: a rough texture has an uneven pattern of highlights and shadows. For this reason, a rough surface attracts the viewer's eyes more easily than a smooth, even surface

tint (tint), *noun* Any hue blended with white

transparent (trans' per ənt), *adj.* Allows light to pass through so objects on the other side can be seen

U

unity (ū' ni tē), *noun* The feeling of wholeness or oneness that is achieved by properly using the elements and principles in art

unrealistic scale (un' rē ə lis' tik skāl), *noun* When an artist makes size relationships that do not make sense

V

value (val' ū), *noun* The lightness or darkness of a hue

value contrast (val' ū kon' trast), *noun* The lightness or darkness stands out from the value that surrounds it

vanishing point (vân' ish' ing point), *noun* The point on the horizon line where all parallel receding lines meet

variety (və ri' ə tē), *noun* The principle of art which is concerned with difference or contrast

vertical (vür' tə kəl), *noun* Lines that move from top to bottom

visual movement (vizh' ü əl müv' mənt), *noun* Created by repeating an art element or object in a work of art

visual rhythm (vizh' ü əl rith' əm), *noun* The repetition of shapes, colors, or lines in a work of art

visual texture (vizh' ü əl teks' chər), *noun* Or simulated texture, imitates real texture. It is texture if we can see how it feels.

W

warm colors (wōrm' kul' ərz), *noun* Red, yellow, and orange. They suggest warmth and come forward toward the viewer.

Z

zigzag (zig' zag) *noun* (adj.) Lines that are made by joining diagonal lines

Index

Photo Credits

36 From the Girard Foundation Collection, in the Museum of International Folk Art, a unit of the Museum of New Mexico, Santa Fe, New Mexico. Photographer: Michel Monteaux; 37 Albright-Knox Art Gallery, Buffalo, New York. Gift of Seymour H. Knox, Jr. 1956. ©Artist Rights Society (ARS), New York; 38 ©Eclipse Studios; 40 High Museum of Art, Atlanta, Georgia, Anonymous gift, 1979.4; 42 ©Eclipse Studios; 43 Randy Ellett; 44 Norton Museum of Art, Gift of R.H. Norton, 47.46. ©Artist Rights Society (ARS), New York/ADAGP, Paris; 45 Helen Birch Bartlett Memorial Collection, 1926.252. Photograph ©2001, The Art Institute of Chicago, All Rights Reserved; 46 ©Eclipse Studios; 47 The Metropolitan Museum of Art, Gift of Mr. and Mrs. Richard Rodgers, 1964. Photography ©1993 The Metropolitan Museum of Art; 48 Smithsonian American Art Museum, Washington, DC. ©2004 Elizabeth Catlett/Licensed By VAGA, New York, NY; 49 National Gallery of Art, Washington, DC. Chester Dale Collection; 51 Randy Ellett; 54 Eclipse Studios; 55 Randy Ellett; 56 Amon Carter Museum, Fort Worth, Texas. P1983.17, ©1981 Aperture Foundation, Inc. Paul Strand Archive; 57 ©Digital Image The Museum of Modern Art/Licensed by SCALA / Art Resource, NY. Photography by Ansel Adams. Used with permission of the Trustees of the Ansel Adams Publishing Rights Trust. All Rights Reserved; 58 ©Eclipse Studios; 60 The Joseph Winterbotham Collection, 1937.166. Reproduction, The Art Institute of Chicago. ©Artist Rights Society (ARS), New York/ADAGP, Paris; 62 Joseph Sohm/ChromoShom/Corbis; 63 Catherine Muga; 64 ©Isabella Stewart Gardner Museum, Boston, Massachusetts, USA/Bridgeman Art Library; 65 ©Erich Lessing/Art Resource, New York; 66, 67 The Museum of Modern Art, New York. Gift of Celeste Bartos. ©Artist Rights Society (ARS), New York/ADAGP, Paris; 68 ©Eclipse Studios; 69 Randy Ellett; 70 Wadsworth Atheneum, Hartford. The Ella Gallup Summer and Mary Catlin Sumner Collection Fund; 71 Gift of Mrs. William E. Scripps. Photograph © 1996 The Detroit Institute of Arts; 73 Randy Ellett; 74 Lent by Willard Straight Hall; Gift of Leonard K. Elmhirst, Class of 1921. Courtesy of the Herbert F. Johnson Museum of Art, Cornell University; 75 ©Frederick Brosen/Forum Gallery; 76 ©Matt Meadows; 78 Courtesy of the Phyllis Kind Gallery; 82 Los Angeles County Museum of Art, Gift of Anna Bing Arnold. ©2004 Artist Rights Society (ARS), New York/ADAGP, Paris; 83 Founders Society Purchase with funds from W. Hawkins Ferry and Mr. Mrs. Walter Buhl Ford II Fund, Eleanor Clay Ford Fund, Marie and Alex Manoogian Fund and members of the Friends of Modern Art. Photograph © The Detroit Institute of Arts; 84 ©Eclipse Studios; 85 Randy Ellett; 88 ©Eclipse Studios; 89 Randy Ellett; 90 Digital Image ©The Museum of Modern Art/Licensed by SCALA/Art Resource, NY; 92 Photodisc/Getty Images, Inc; 97 ©2004 Artist Rights Society (ARS), New York/ADAGP, Paris; 98 ©Eclipse Studios; 99 Randy Ellett; 100 The Art Institute of Chicago. Gift of Georgia O'Keeffe. ©2004 The Georgia O'Keeffe Foundation/Artist Rights Society (ARS), New York; 103 Randy Ellett; 106 ©Eclipse Studios; 107 Randy Ellett; 108 The New Orleans Museum of Art; On loan from the Mrs. Frederick M. Stafford Collection. ©2004 Artist Rights Society (ARS), New York/ADAGP, Paris; 110 ©Eclipse Studios; 112, 113 International Folk Art Foundation Collection. Museum of International Folk Art. Santa Fe, New Mexico. Photo by: Pat Pollard; 114 ©Eclipse Studios; 115 Randy Ellett; 116 High Museum of Art, Atlanta, Georgia, Virginia Carroll Crawford Collection, 1982.291; 117 Purchased with funds provided by the Smithsonian Collections Acquisition Program. Photograph by Frank Khoury. National Museum of African Art, Smithsonian Institution, Washington D.C; 118 ©Eclipse Studios; 119 Randy Ellett; 120 ©SCALA/Art Resource, NY. Pushkin Museum of Fine Arts, Moscow; 122 Bob Krist/Corbis; 123 Michal Daniel; 124 The Nelson-Atkins Museum of Art, Kansas City, Missouri (Gift of Byron and Eileen Cohen); 125 Complimentary Trish Bransten; 126 Muskegon Museum of Art, Hackley Picture Fund. 35.4; 128 ©Eclipse Studios; 130 The Metropolitan Museum of Art, The Jules Bache Collection, 1949. Photograph ©1978 The Metropolitan Museum of Art; 131 The Metropolitan Museum of Art, Purchase, Rogers Fund and The Kevorkian Foundation Gift, 1955. Photograph ©1980 The Metropolitan Museum of Art; 134 ©2004 Elizabeth Catlett/Licensed By VAGA, New York, NY; 135 Gift of Beaux Arts. The Lowe Art Museum, The University of Miami, Coral Gables, Florida; 136 ©Eclipse Studios; 143 The Metropolitan Museum of Art, The Michael C. Rockefeller Memorial Collection, Bequest of Nelson A. Rockefeller, 1979. Photograph ©1997 The Metropolitan Museum of Art; 145 Randy Ellett; 147 Art ©Estate of Duane Hanson/Licensed by VAGA, New York, NY; 148 ©Eclipse Studios; 150 Norton Museum of Art, West Palm Beach, Florida, Bequest of R.H. Norton, 53.26. ©2004 Artist Rights Society (ARS), New York/ADAGP, Paris; 153 Photo Max Waldman/©Max Waldman Archives; 156 International Folk Art Foundation Collection. Museum of International Folk Art. Santa Fe, New Mexico. Photo by: John Bigelow Taylor; 157 ©Smithsonian American Art Museum/Art Resource, NY; 158 (tl) ©Getty Images, Inc, (tr) ©Photodisc/Getty Images, Inc, 158 (b) ©Eclipse Studios; 159 Randy Ellett; 160 ©The Museum of Modern of Art, New York/Licensed by Scala/Art Resource, NY; 161 ©Art Resource, NY; 162 ©Eclipse Studios; 163 Randy Ellett; 164 ©The Museum of Modern Art, New York/Licensed by Scala/Art Resource, NY; 165 ©The Museum of Modern Art, New York/Licensed by Scala/Art Resource, NY. ©Estate of Pablo Picasso/Artist Rights Society (ARS), New York; 166 ©Eclipse Studios; 167 Randy Ellett; 168 Arthur M. Sackler Gallery, Smithsonian Institution, Washington, D.C.: Purchase - Smithsonian Collections Acquisition Program and partial gift of Richard G. Prtizlaff; 169 Los Angeles County Museum of Art, Los Angeles County Fund. Photo ©1999 Museum Associates, LACMA; 170 (l) ©Photodisc/Getty Images, Inc, (r) ©Getty Images, Inc; 171 Randy Ellett; 172 Art Resource, NY; 174 ©Eclipse Studios; 175 Randy Ellett; 178 (l) Steve Lupton/Corbis, (r) Charles & Josette Lenars/Corbis, (b) ©Eclipse Studios; 179 Randy Ellett; 182 Herbert Migdoll; 184 Gift of Mrs. Charles S. Carstairs, Image ©2003 Board of Trustees, National Gallery of Art, Washington; 185 ©Corbis Sygma; 186 ©T.H. Benton and R.P. Benton Testamentary Trusts/Licensed By VAGA, New York, NY; 188 ©Eclipse Studios; 189, 190 Randy Ellett; 191 Archive Center,